# DEATH and ART

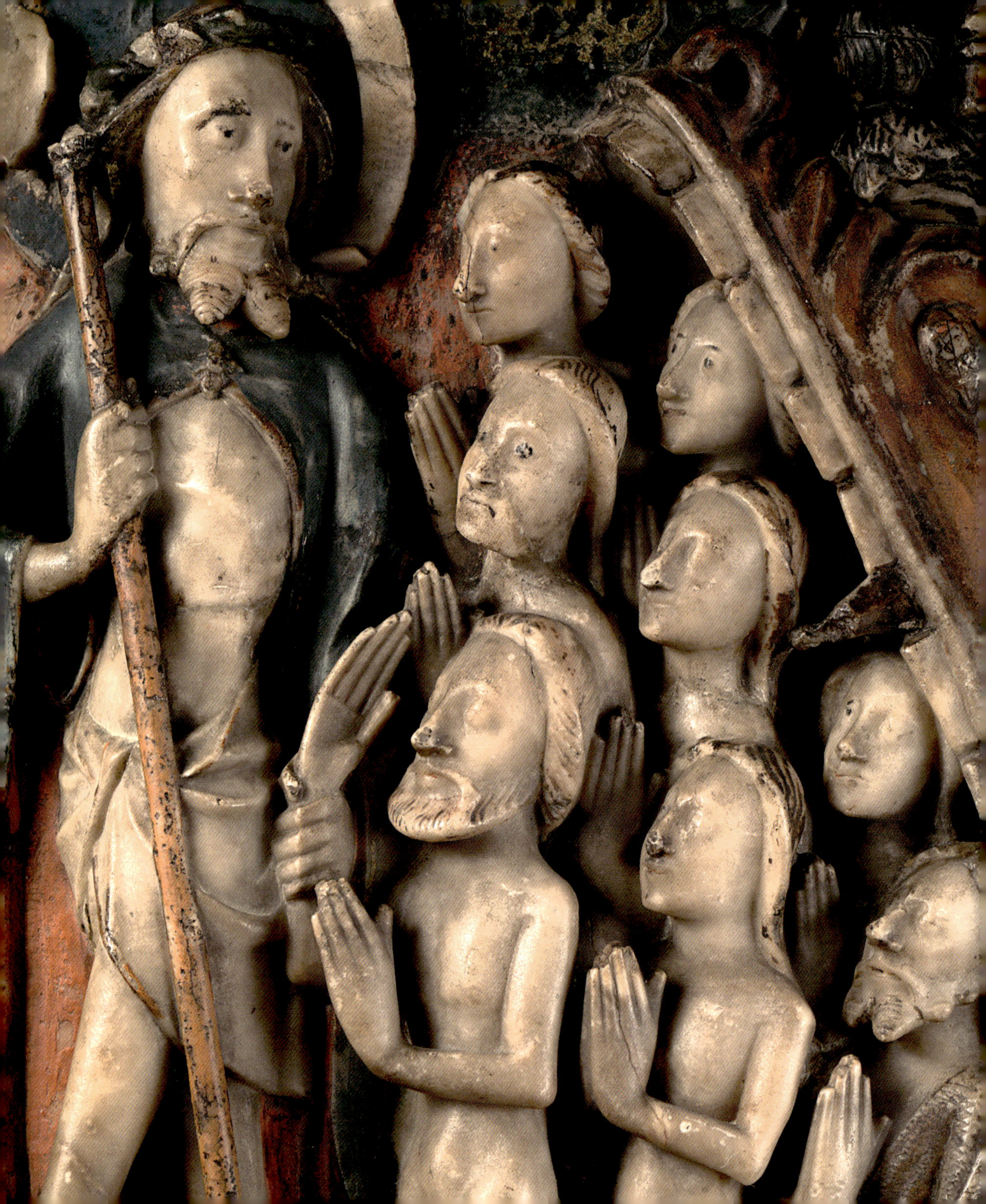

# DEATH and ART

## EUROPE 1200–1530

Eleanor Townsend

V&A Publishing

First published by V&A Publishing, 2009

V&A Publishing
Victoria and Albert Museum
South Kensington
London SW7 2RL


Distributed in North America by Harry N. Abrams, Inc., New York



ISBN: 978 1 85177 583 5
Library of Congress Catalog Control Number: 2009923086

10 9 8 7 6 5 4 3 2 1
2013 2012 2011 2010 2009

A catalogue record for this book is available from the British Library.



Designed by Andrew Shoolbred

Jacket (detail) and flaps: *Emblems of the Church* (rear flap) *and Laity* (front flap and jacket), stained
glass, Normandy (France), *c*.1500–30 (V&A: C.75 and C.76–1953). These two panels were once placed
either side of a window showing the Triumph of Death, probably in Saint-Herbland, Rouen.
Back jacket: *Weighing of Souls*, stained glass, England, 1500–50 (V&A: C.164–1929)
Frontispiece: *The Harrowing of Hell* (detail of plate 9).

All quotations have been modernized and translated where necessary.

Printed in China

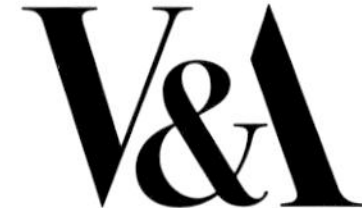

V&A Publishing
Victoria and Albert Museum
South Kensington
London SW7 2RL
www.vam.ac.uk

# Contents

For FRJB and AGFB

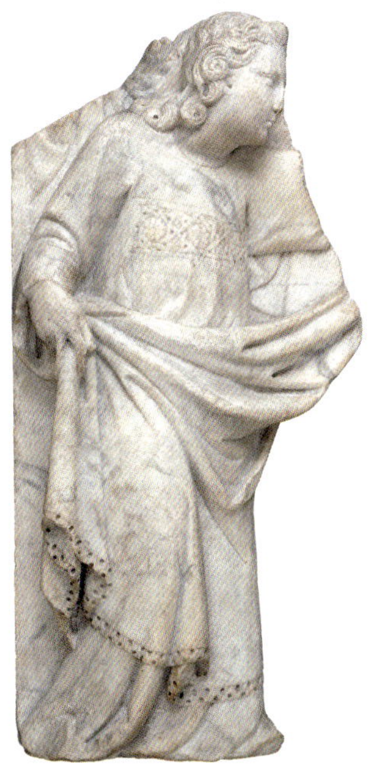



John Burgoyne's will, 1540

# Introduction



Medieval people had a far more direct experience of death than most of us today. Even during periods without plague or famine, death rates remained high, often three times those of modern developed countries, and the average life expectancy was about half today's rate.

The experience of the Black Death – the plague that swept Europe from Hungary and Italy to England and Iceland in recurring waves from 1348 onwards – was clearly shattering for those who lived through it. An estimated one-third of the population died, with almost total annihilation in some areas. Almost all western Europeans in this period were Christians and followed the teachings of the Catholic Church. Death was far from being simply the end, but rather the beginning of a whole new journey into the afterlife. This could be prepared for during life, and could be eased by ensuring a 'good death'. The terror of the Black Death reinforced the interest of the laity in preparing for this moment. Describing the situation in Avignon in 1348, an anonymous Flemish cleric wrote:

> Neither kinsmen nor friends visit the sick. Priests do not hear the confessions of the sick, or administer the sacraments to them. Everyone who is still healthy looks after himself. So it happens every day that a rich man is carried to his grave by . . . ruffians, with just a few lights and no mourners.

The fear of dying without a priest, or of being interred in a mass burial without the essential prayers for one's soul, weighed on the minds of many.

Such attitudes are clear from many of the artefacts that remain to us from the thirteenth to sixteenth centuries. Images of the Last Judgement, Heaven, Hell and Purgatory reflect a debate over these concepts that only gradually reached some sort of consensus. There were clear-cut variations between what the Church taught, what people believed on a local level and what was depicted in works of art.

The subject matter chosen to illustrate prayer books and decorate personal devotional objects shows a concern with establishing a relationship with the saints, Christ and the Virgin, as well as proving one's piety by commissioning religious works of art. *Memento mori*, in which Death figures remind the viewer that death comes to all, became increasingly popular (plate 1). Tombs and memorials focused largely on soliciting prayers from the living to help the soul of the dead person on its onward journey. The overwhelming impression is of a society where the increasingly wealthy urban classes, as well as the nobility, had money to spend on saving their souls, and good reason to do so.

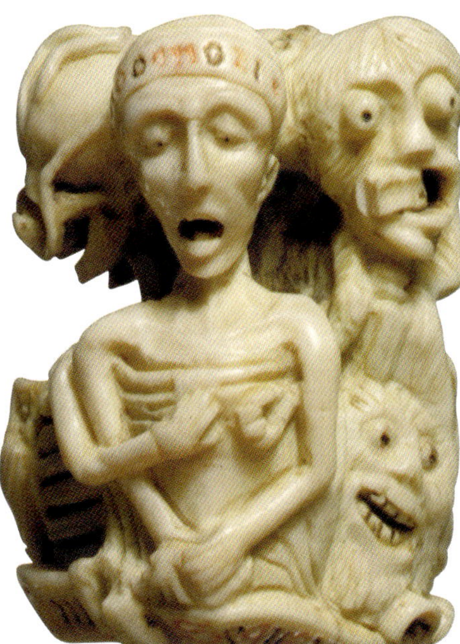
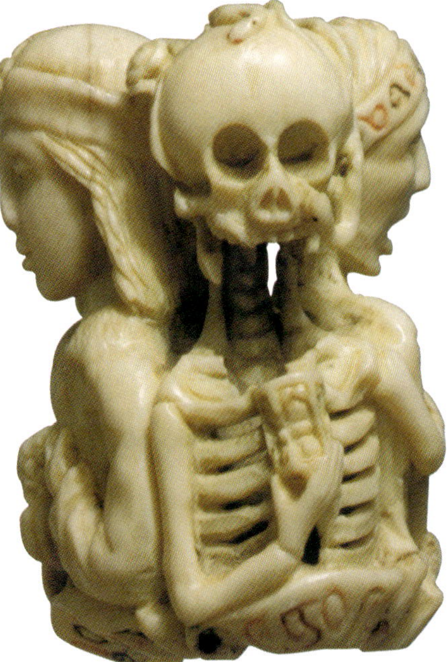

1

Two sides of a rosary bead, showing a dying man with a devil pulling at him (below left), and a skeleton with an hourglass (below right); ivory with traces of paint, possibly France, *c.*1525–50

(V&A: 2149–1855)

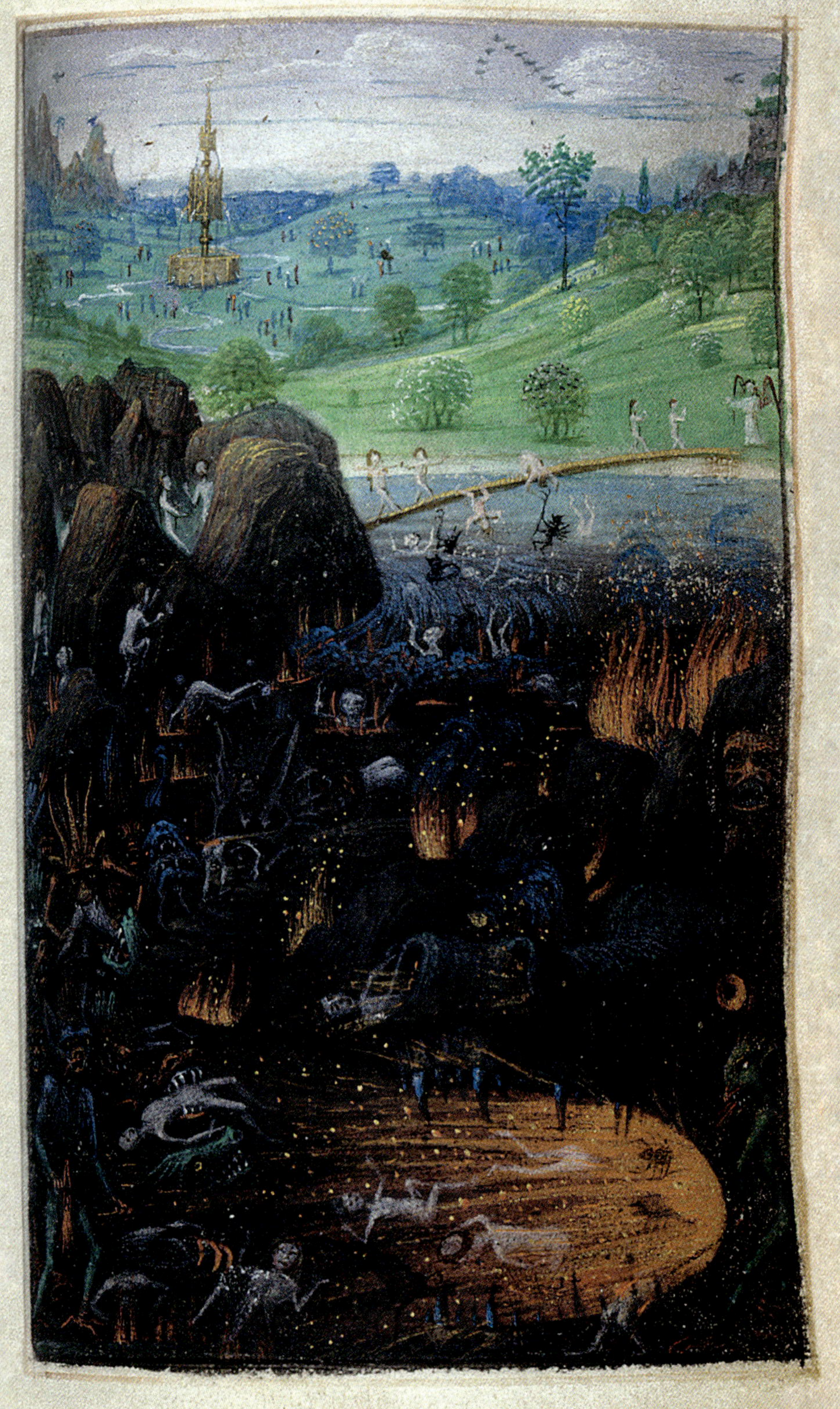

# CHAPTER I

# *Life after death*

To the medieval Christian mind, life after death was almost as real as the everyday world. Graphic images of the afterlife, based largely on written texts, were available to all in wall paintings and sculpted church portals. Small-scale ivories and illuminated manuscripts spelt out the soul's eventual fate to wealthy patrons. Death was the beginning of an onward journey with an ultimate destination that was far from certain (plate 3). Over the centuries the great theologians debated exactly what could be expected. Finally some sort of consensus began to appear in the 1200s, though even this was not universally accepted, and several of the key beliefs were subject to confusion in visual terms.

The geography of the afterlife was described very specifically in numerous texts, ranging from the vision of the Northumbrian layman Drycthelm, as

2 OPPOSITE
Heaven and Hell, from a book of hours, by the Painter of Fitzwilliam 268; illuminated manuscript, Bruges (Belgium), c. 1480
(V&A: MSL/1910/2384, f.153)

Hell is at the bottom, with Limbo the rocky area to the left. Souls cross a bridge as a form of Purgatory, before reaching the garden of Heaven with the golden Fountain of Life.

3 RIGHT
Life after death, as taught by the Catholic Church from the mid-13th century

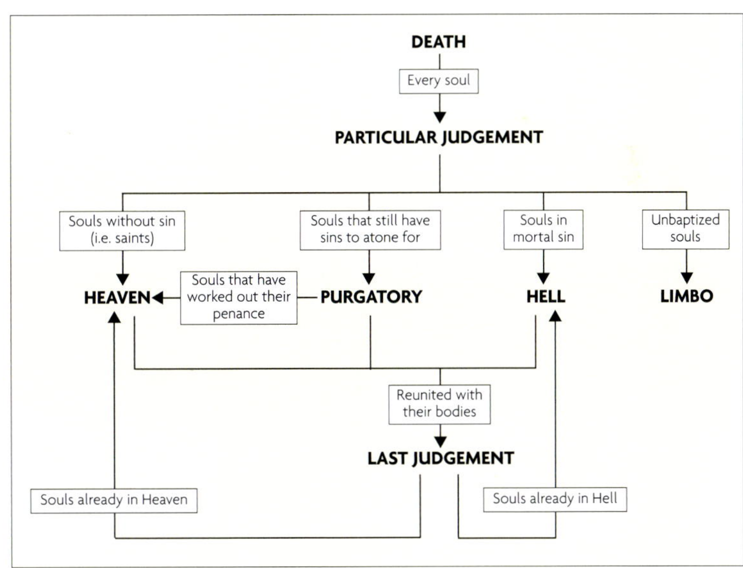

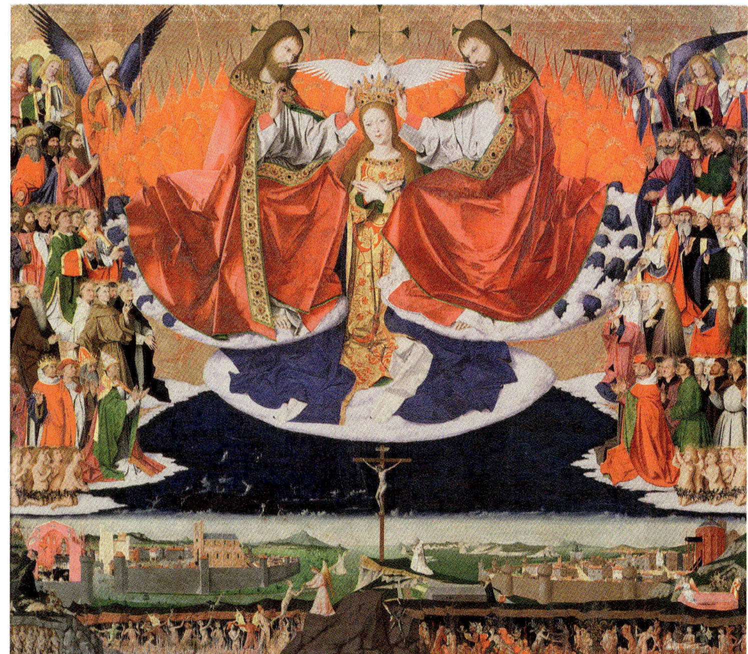

4

*Coronation of the Virgin*, by Enguerrand Quarton; tempera on panel, Avignon (France), *c.*1453

(Musée Pierre de Luxembourg, Villeneuve-lès-Avignon, France)

The upper part shows the Virgin crowned by the Holy Trinity in Heaven, represented by ranks of saints and angels. Below is Earth, and below that on the left is Purgatory and on the right, Hell.

recounted by Bede in the eighth century, to Dante's *Divine Comedy* in the fourteenth. Such descriptions varied radically in their detail, but everyone agreed on two final destinations for the soul: Heaven or Hell. This dualistic view had its roots in Judaism, and also reflected ancient Greek and Roman beliefs. Following these traditions, Heaven was seen as 'up' and Hell as 'down', a feature of many medieval representations (plate 4). Both concepts were eternal: once the soul was in either place, it was there for ever.

## HEAVEN

*Her light was like unto a stone most precious, even like a jasper stone, clear as crystal*
Revelation 21:11

Christians in the later Middle Ages had several models for Heaven, which appeared in both textual and visual sources. It was sometimes depicted as a garden, a view that lent itself to the imagination of artists (see plate 2). This also provided a visual link to the Garden of Eden (the Earthly Paradise from which Adam and Eve had been expelled). The detailed description in Genesis (2:8–14) suggested that the Garden of Eden was a geographical place, and it often featured

5
*Mappa Mundi* (Map of the World),
by Richard of Haldingham and
Lafford; illuminated manuscript,
England, *c.*1300

(Hereford Cathedral Library)

The map shows east at the top. The
Garden of Eden is shown in a circle at
the top, just inside the main circle of
the world.

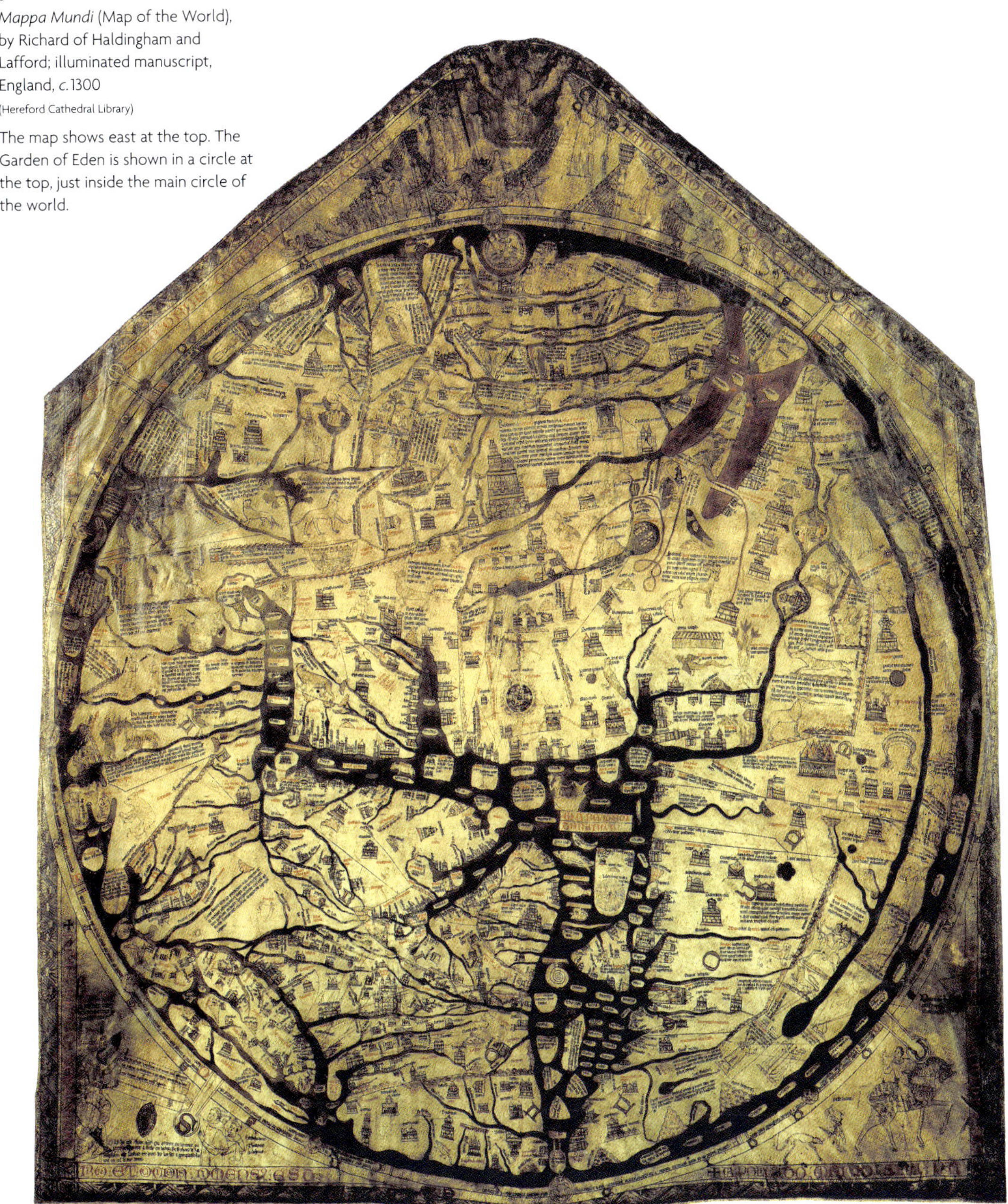

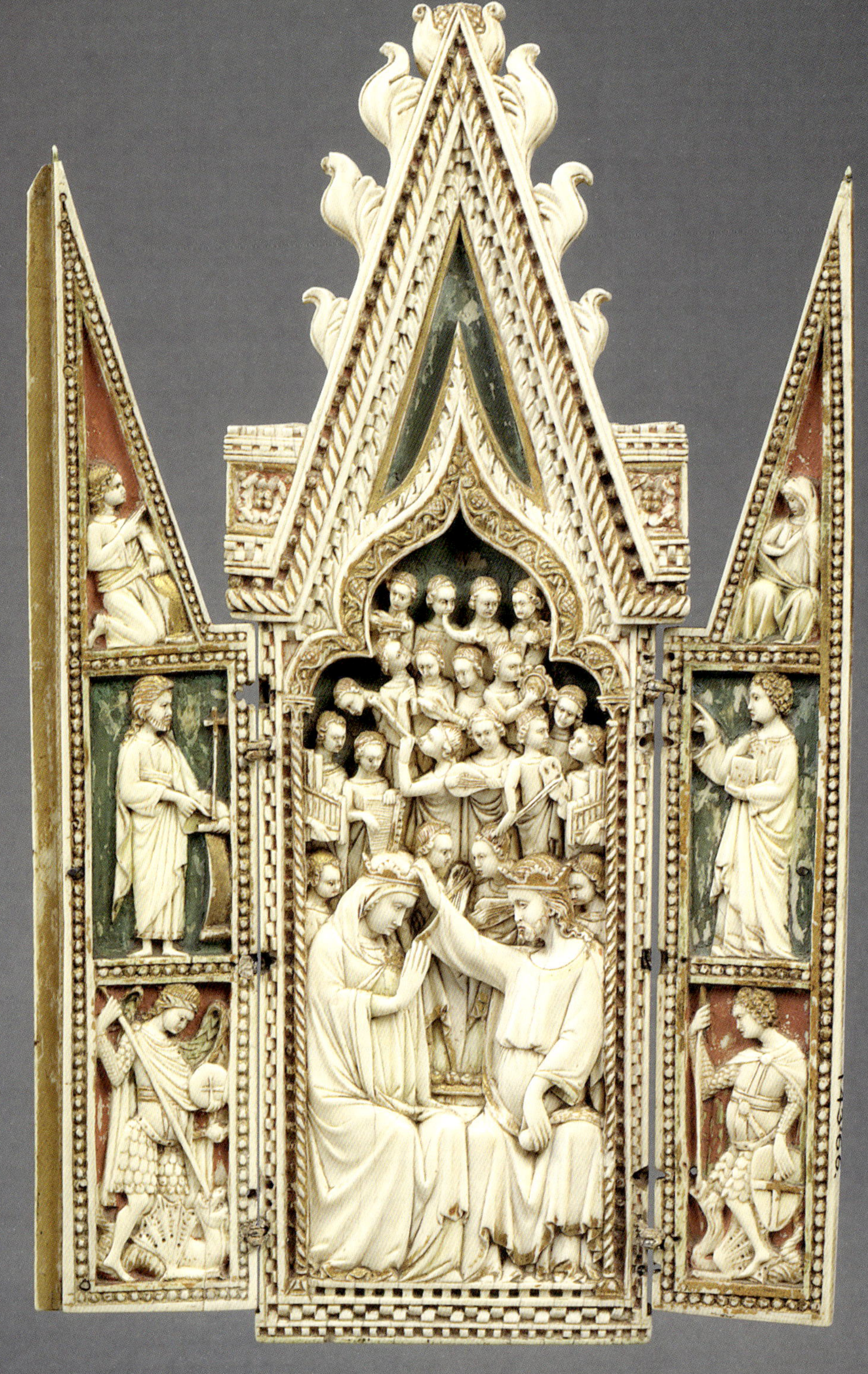

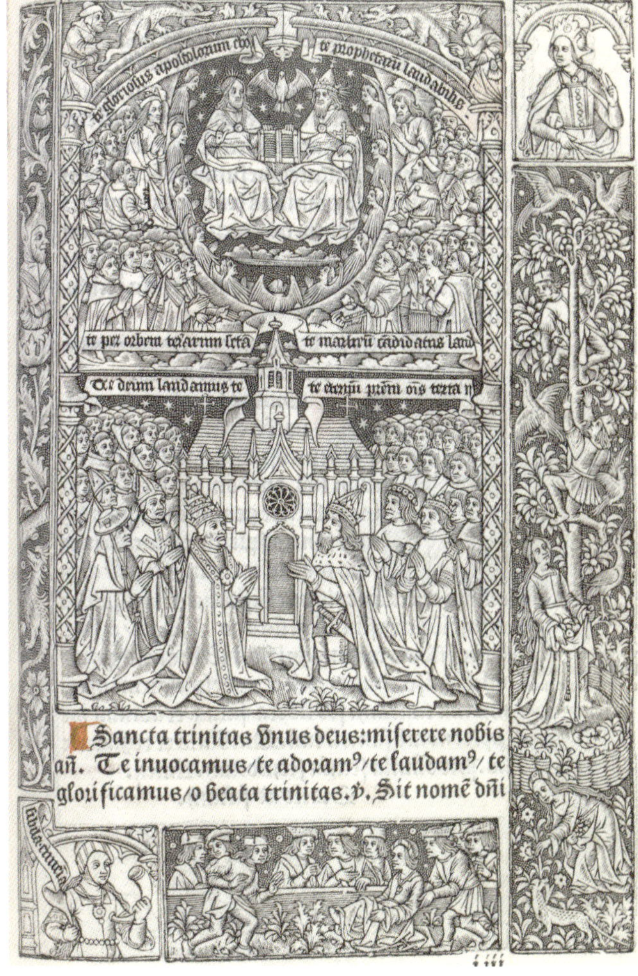

on contemporary maps (plate 5). It was distinct from the Celestial Paradise, where God dwelt with his saints and angels. Another view of Heaven followed the description in Revelation of the 'holy city, new Jerusalem' (Revelation 21:2) and showed it as a great city. And often it was simply represented by the presence of the figure of God the Father, surrounded by ranks of saints, martyrs and angels (plate 6), frequently bathed in golden light or with a star-sprinkled background (plate 7). Heaven was reunion with God himself.

## HELL



Depictions of Hell were more consistent. They stressed the darkness and eternal fire described in the Bible, as well as a range of ingenious tortures, often with punishments tailor-made to fit the sin. Medieval thinkers were fascinated by detail: an *Apocalypse* said to have been written by St Paul declared that there were exactly 144,000 tortures. 'In place of scented baths . . . there they shall have a bath more foul than any bath of pitch and sulphur,' wrote John Bromyard in his *Summa Predecantium* of around 1300, 'instead of wives, they shall have toads.' Dante, in his great vision of life after death, *The Divine Comedy* (c.1307–21), describes in ghastly detail (Inferno, 28:24–7) the fate of those who spread dissension and scandal:

> . . . One whom I
> Saw ripped right from his chin to where we fart:
> Bowels hung between his legs, one saw
> His vitals and the miserable sack
> That makes of what we swallow excrement.

These horrors were illustrated all too literally in numerous editions of the famous text (plate 8). Hell's torments are sometimes also shown within the wide gaping jaws of an unnamed monster (see plate 9). The depictions of the jaws of Hell, or hell mouth, derived ultimately from Old Testament descriptions of the monster, Leviathan (Job 41).

## RESURRECTION AND LAST JUDGEMENT



At the end of time, all the souls of the dead would be physically reunited with their bodies at the Resurrection. The soul needed its body at this point to experience the full effects of retribution, or the bliss of reunion with God in Heaven.

Like the Resurrection, the idea of a Last Judgement at the end of time had firm biblical authority and was consistently reinforced by the Church. As a result,

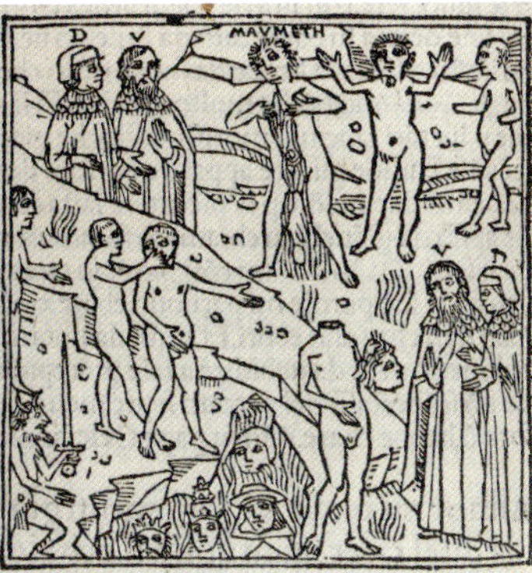

8 ABOVE
Hell, from Dante's *Divine Comedy*;
woodcut, printed by Bartholomeo de
Zanni da Portese, Venice (Italy), 1507
(V&A: 38041800159915, f. cxv)

9 RIGHT
The Harrowing of Hell; alabaster,
England, 15th century
(V&A: A.1–1955)

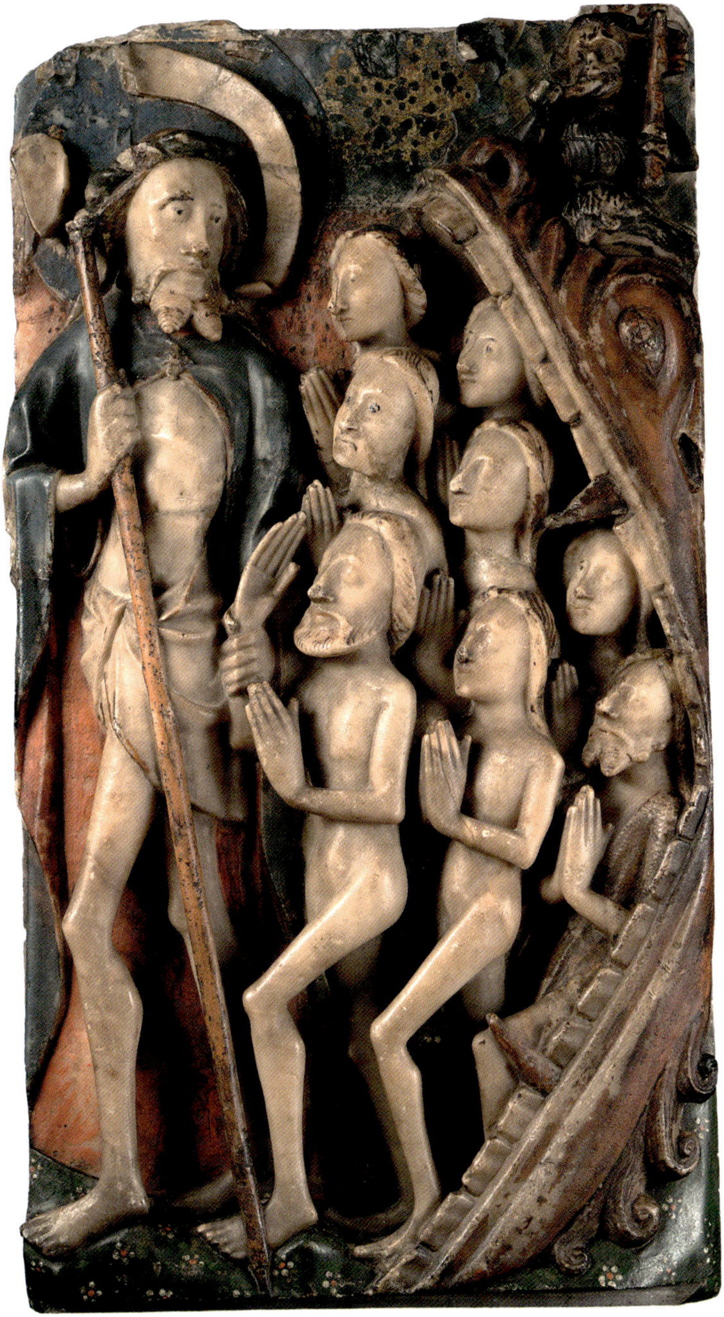

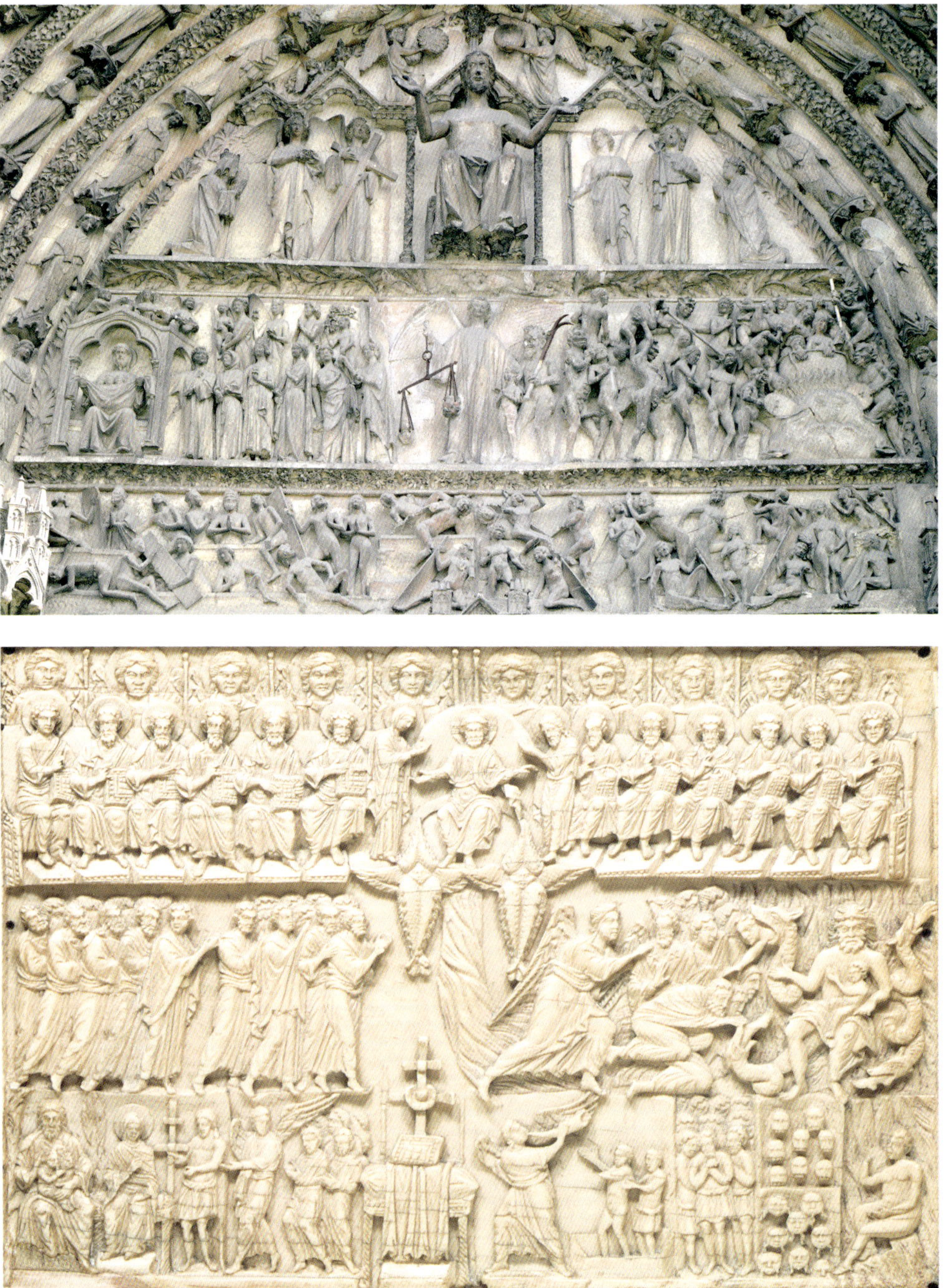

the main elements of visual representations remain remarkably constant over time, appearing in a variety of media and on both a large and small scale (plate 10 and plate 11). Christ is shown, sitting as the all-powerful judge, flanked by the Virgin and St John the Evangelist or St John the Baptist, who would intercede for the souls of the dead. These souls are often seen below in the process of resurrection. Angels usher the saved to Heaven on the left, while the damned are dragged to Hell on the right.

Some believed that this terrible day would be preceded by apocalyptic disasters to herald the end of the world. The anonymous English poem, *The Pricke of Conscience*, set out what would happen each day, and the dramatic events were illustrated in printed books of hours (plate 12) and other media.

## LIMBO

> There lament is not an outcry,
> but a sigh
>
> Dante, *Purgatorio* 7:30

The years around 1200 saw a major reorganization of the agreed geography of the afterlife. The idea of Limbo emerged fully at around this date. This was a third place, usually seen as a section of Hell but without its terrible suffering, intended for the unbaptized. One part was occupied by worthy figures that lived before the time of Christ, including Abraham and the prophets. Dante includes classical figures, such as Homer and Virgil. This Limbo of the Fathers was the setting for the popular image of the Harrowing of Hell (see plate 9). Based on the apocryphal gospel of Nicodemus, and a feature particularly of Byzantine iconography, the story told how Christ visited Hell after his crucifixion, rescuing the unbaptized 'worthies' and sealing the rest of Hell for eternity. The remaining part of Limbo contains the souls of unbaptized babies: 'those whom the teeth of death hath seized before / They were set

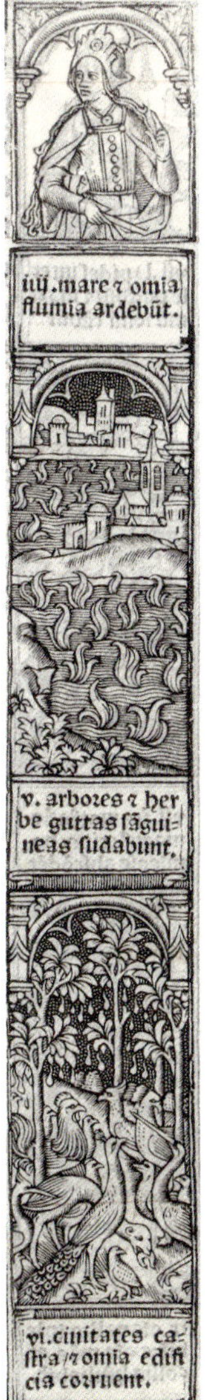

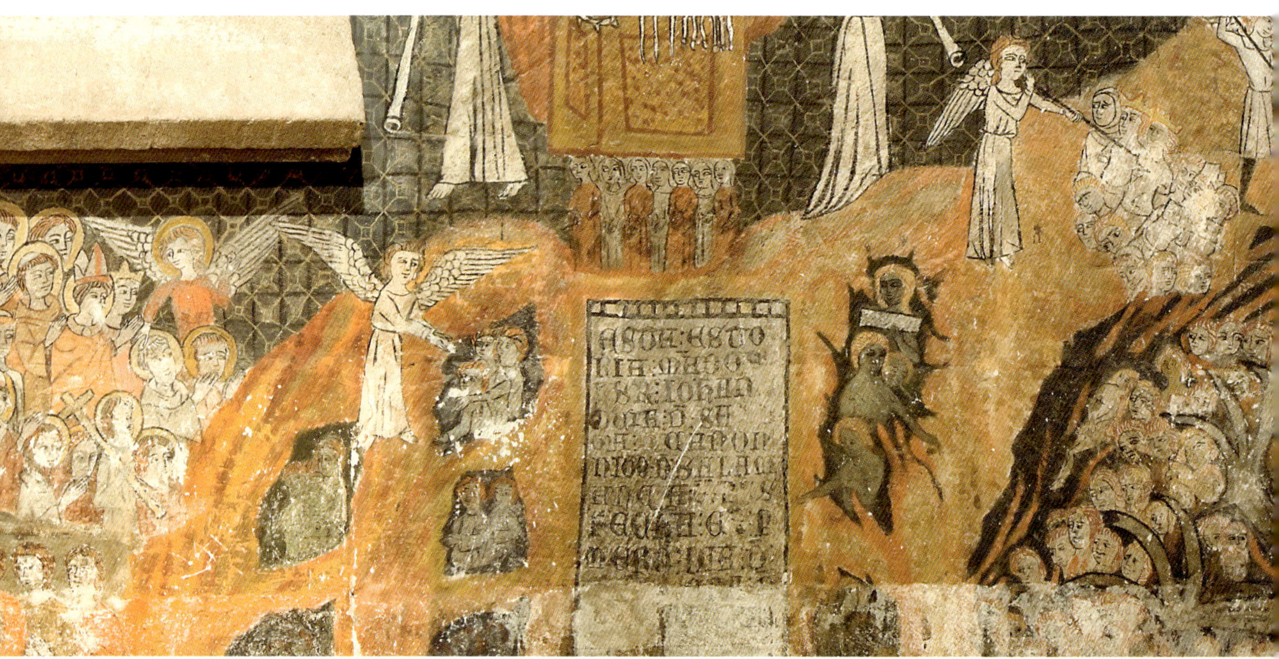

13
Heaven, Purgatory, Limbo and Hell;
wall painting, Spain, early 14th
century
(Old Cathedral, Salamanca, Spain)

Souls in Limbo are shown in the
enclosed cells to the right of
the inscription.

free from human sinfulness' (Dante, *Purgatorio* 7:22–3). There are relatively few representations of the Limbo of the Innocents, but those that do survive – which are found from Spain to Transylvania (plate 13) – reflect a belief that was accepted right across Europe.

## THE ARRIVAL OF PURGATORY

From the early days of the Christian Church there was debate over what happened to the souls of the dead between death and the end of time. Until about 1200 the most popular answer was provided by the story of Lazarus the beggar, who 'was carried by the angels into Abraham's bosom' (Luke 16:22) after death. This was seen as a place of comfort, depicted in art by the figure of Abraham as an old bearded man cradling one or more souls in a napkin (see plate 14).

Very gradually, from the time of St Augustine (354–430) onwards, a new theory began to gain currency across Christendom. This suggested that, on death, the soul of a person who was neither supremely good nor supremely bad would enter a period of purging. This was to atone for sins committed during life, and would enable the person to enter Heaven. The word *purgatorium*, or Purgatory, seems to have appeared for the first time at the end of the twelfth century, but the Church did not accept it fully until the mid-1200s.

Only saints went straight to Heaven, and only those found guilty of terrible sins went straight to Hell. Most people expected to spend some time in Purgatory and were therefore fascinated by the minutest details. The relationship between purgatorial time and earthly time attracted the attention of various authorities. Accounts were published of apparitions appearing to relatives to announce that the deceased's stay in Purgatory was complete – these usually occurred just months or even days after death. The inference was that, although time spent in Purgatory was short in earthly terms, it seemed like many years to the suffering soul.

There was also interest in its precise physical location: entrances to Purgatory were believed to exist in both Ireland and Sicily. And of course the specific nature of the punishments to be expected there was much discussed. It was generally agreed that the 'said pain of Purgatory is more grievous, an hundred thousand double than that of this present world' (*The Arte and Crafte to Lyve Well*, printed by Wynkyn de Worde, 1505), and the punishments were said to have the same ingenious variation as awaited souls in Hell. 'There the lazy will be driven with burning prongs, and gluttons tormented

14
Monumental brass of Abraham or God the Father, with souls in a napkin; brass and enamel, France, 15th century
(V&A: M.69–1949)

15
Purgatory, from a fragmentary
book of hours; illuminated
manuscript, Netherlands, *c*.1490
(V&A: MSL/1668/1902, f.1)

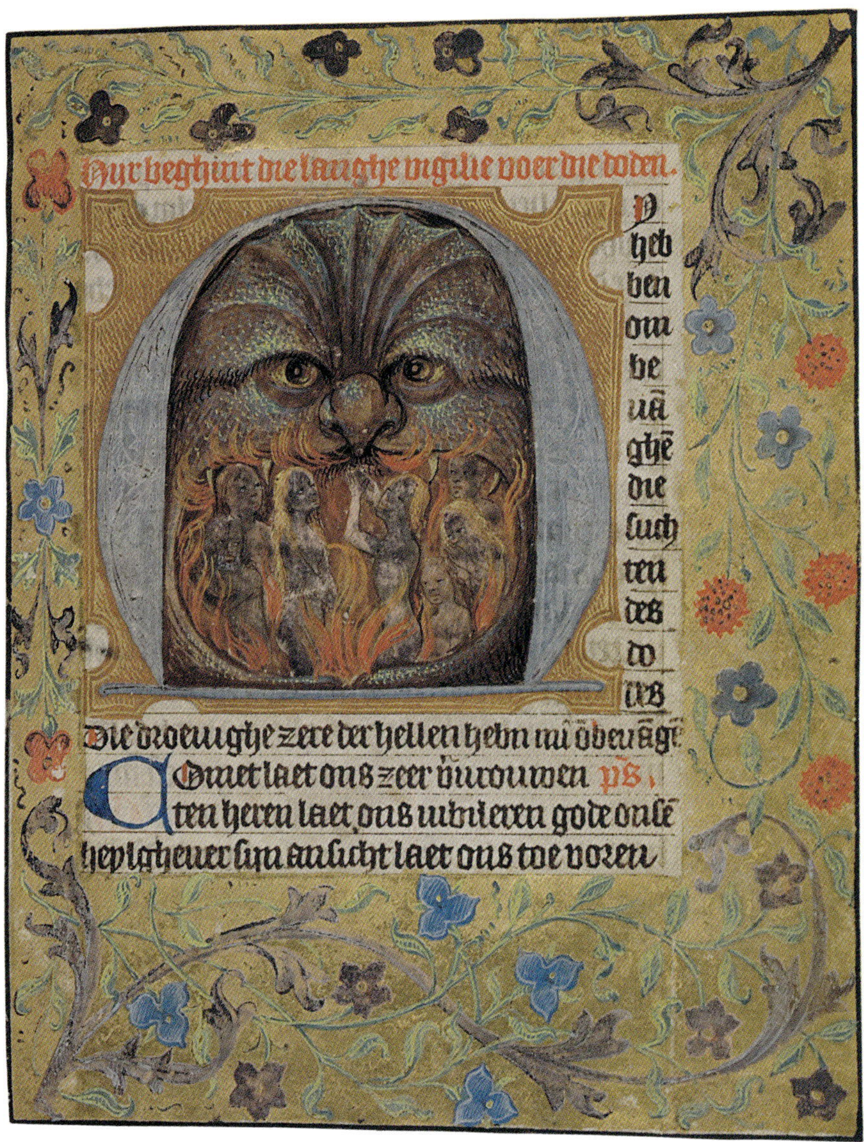

with unspeakable hunger and thirst: the wanton and lust-loving will be bathed in burning pitch and foul brimstone . . . ' wrote Thomas à Kempis in his popular *Imitation of Christ* (1:24), first published in about 1418. The intensity and length of trial would reflect the seriousness of one's sins in life. But the experience was far more bearable than Hell's torments, because the promise remained of eventual reunion with God.

In spite of this fascination with Purgatory, the concept remained essentially nebulous. The subject therefore never supplanted the Last Judgement as an image of the afterlife for art. Where Purgatory does appear, it is usually depicted in a similar way to Hell with the customary fire and suffering, but with angels removing souls to Heaven, or at least bringing them refreshment and the hope of salvation. Other versions show souls engulfed in flames, but calmly praying for the salvation still available to them (plate 15). The detailed contract for Enguerrand Quarton's painting of the Last Things (plate 4, page 12), which includes a rare depiction of Purgatory, had to specify many features, such as the angel providing refreshment and the inclusion of representatives of different levels of society. This demonstrates the lack of agreed iconography for this subject.

Some images show Purgatory in the form of a bridge or a ladder (for example plate 2, page 10) representing an intermediary stage between the horrors of Hell and the safety of Heaven, through which the soul must pass. Dante also sees Purgatory as a transitional stage: his *Divine Comedy* describes it as a mountain with nine levels, which had to be climbed to reach the nine spheres of Heaven above.

## PARTICULAR JUDGEMENT

As soon as the soul is set free from the body it is either plunged into hell or soars to heaven, unless it be held back by some debt

Supplement to Thomas Aquinas's *Summa Theologica*, late thirteenth century

The advent of Purgatory necessitated an immediate decision after death as to whether the soul would spend time in Purgatory or pass directly to Heaven, Hell or Limbo (see plate 3, page 11). The doctrine of Particular, or Personal, Judgement (distinct from the more general Last Judgement at the end of time) developed to answer this need.

Artists faced problems in depicting the Particular Judgement. Although Christ was still the judge, showing him in judgement of the individual straight after

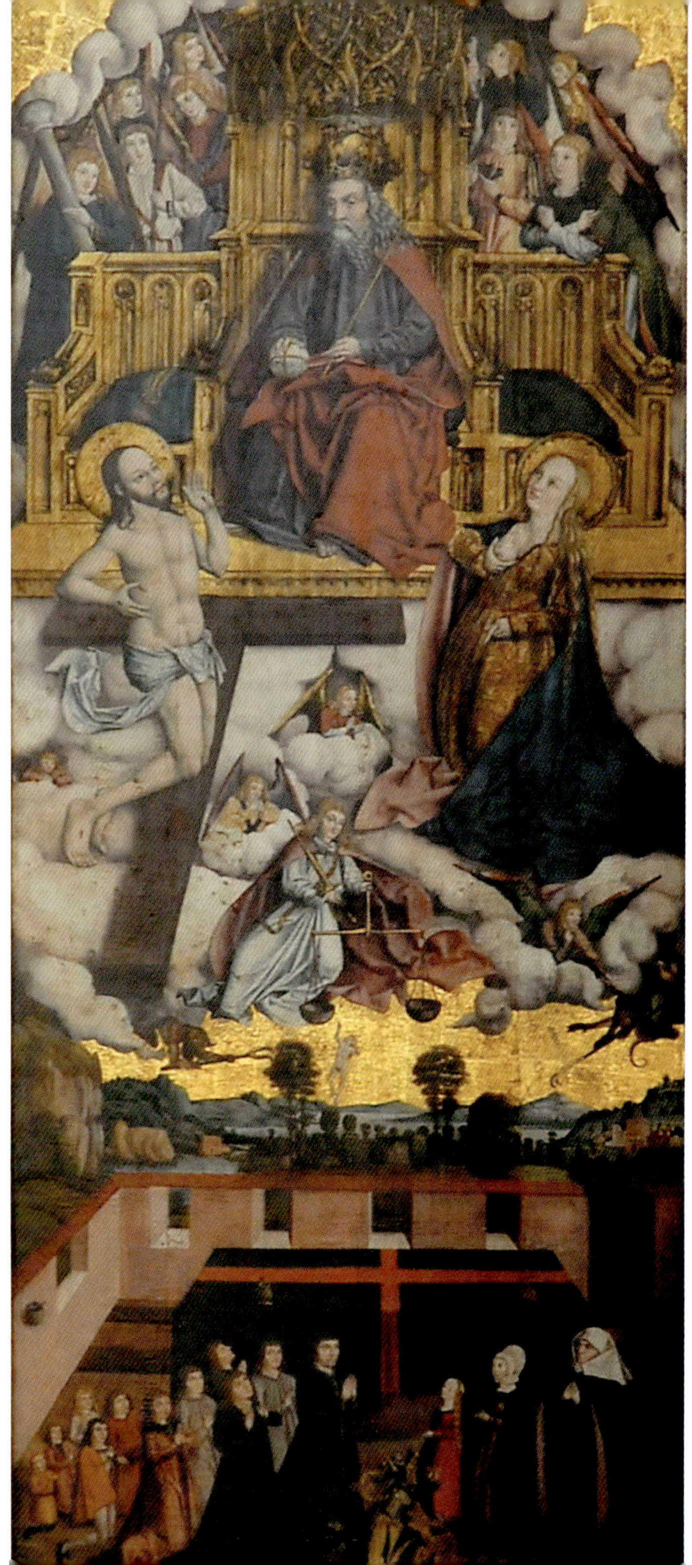

Epitaph of the Scholl family of
Dinkelsbühl, Swabia; oil on panel,
Swabia (Germany), *c.*1500
(St Lambert's church, Erkelenz, Germany)

The tiny soul moves upwards from its
coffin to face Particular Judgement.
Above, St Michael waits with his scales,
while Christ and the Virgin plead for
mercy from God the Father.

death would risk confusion with Last Judgement iconography. The few pictorial representations of this idea are therefore varied in their imagery. Some (for example plate 16) show St Michael the archangel as judge, using his scales to weigh each soul. St Michael was already associated with judgement from appearances in Last Judgement scenes, so it is not surprising to find him taking on this role. In the Scholl epitaph, he acts in conjunction with God the Father. Other representations (for example plate 45, page 52) show a battle between angels and devils for the soul at the moment of death.

Purgatory, and the associated Particular Judgement, enabled mortals to take some measure of control over their eventual fate after death – the concept did not exist simply to terrify and chasten. Long before Purgatory was formalized as part of Christian belief, St Augustine had confirmed that the actions of the living (through prayers, the celebration of the Mass and charitable works) could affect the fate of souls as they journeyed through the afterlife. The full acceptance of the doctrine of Purgatory made this relationship between the living and the dead particularly intense, with critical consequences for the production of art.

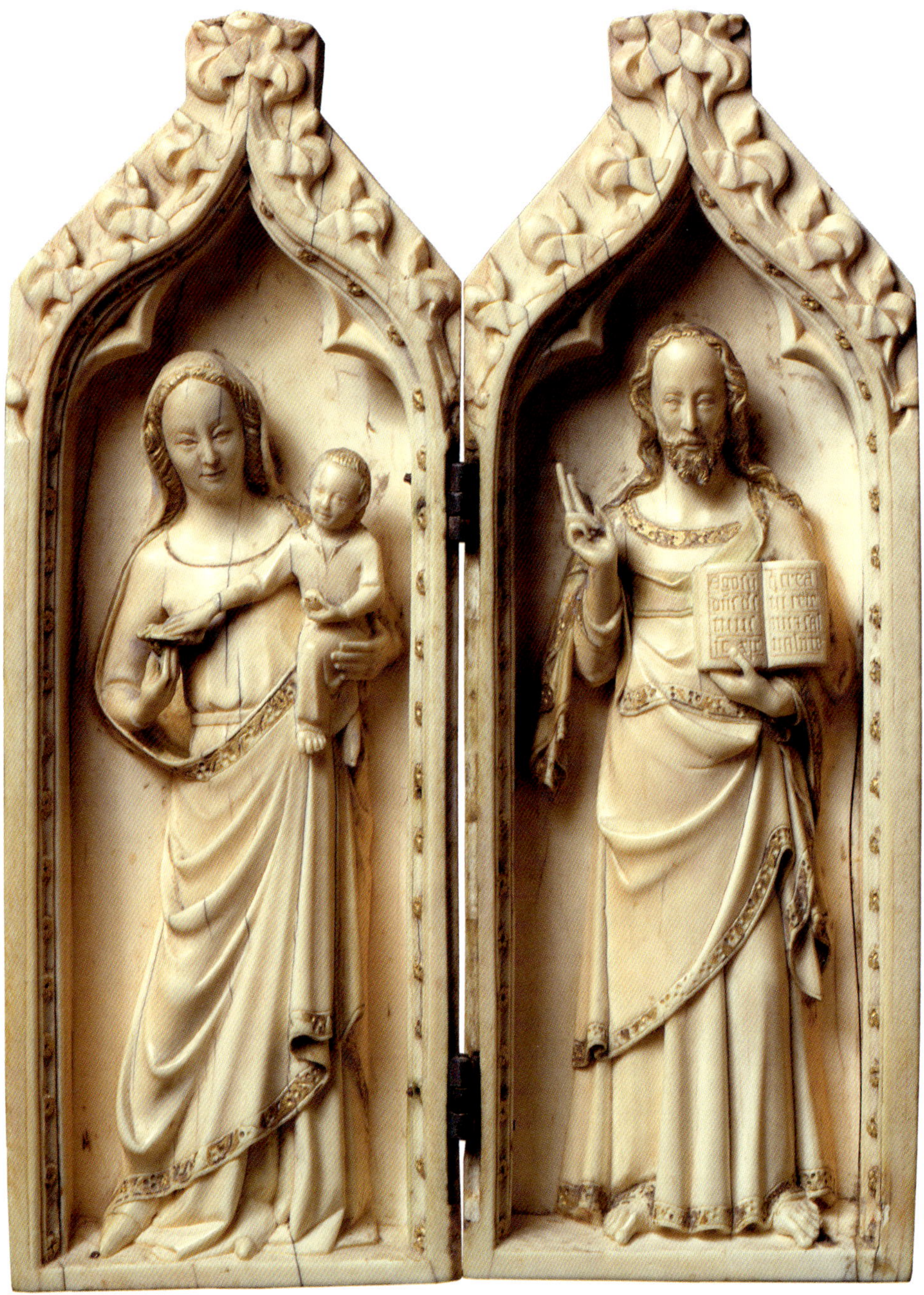

# CHAPTER 2

# In the midst of life, we are in death

As death heralded an ongoing and uncertain journey into the afterlife, most Christians believed that securing the future of their own soul (and those of family and friends) was important. In spite of a clear concern at the horrific torments awaiting some in the afterlife, the late medieval period was far from being doom-laden. As actions in life could affect one's fate after death, everyone had the opportunity to take control of their spiritual future. Many of the methods employed had important consequences for the visual arts.

In essence, the focus of concern was twofold. Firstly, individuals were keen to lessen the time their soul might have to spend in Purgatory. The proper place for purging was on Earth during life, as advised by Thomas à Kempis: 'It is better to atone for sin now and to cut away vices than to keep them for purgation in the hereafter' (*The Imitation of Christ*, 1:24). It was believed that activities, such as penance or good works, undertaken in life were more than twice as effective as relying on one's family and friends to pray for one after death. Secondly, we can see people making arrangements to encourage the living to pray for their soul after they had died. Souls in Purgatory were not able to pray for themselves, so it was important to establish arrangements for the future.

17 OPPOSITE
Diptych with images of the Virgin and Child and Christ; ivory, England, *c.*1310–20
(V&A: A.545–1910)

## GOOD WORKS

Then [at the Last Judgement] holy works will be of greater value than many fair words
Thomas à Kempis, *The Imitation of Christ*, 1:24

The phrase 'good works' covered a range of activities, both practical and spiritual, that devout Christians could undertake to enhance their spiritual well-being and minimize the time their soul might have to spend in Purgatory after death. Practical works might range from almsgiving to improving one's parish church or building roads and bridges. All benefited one's neighbours and were therefore acts of charity. The Church taught that there were Seven Corporal Works of Mercy: to feed the hungry; to give drink to the thirsty; to clothe the naked; to shelter the homeless; to visit the sick; to visit the prisoner; and to bury the dead.

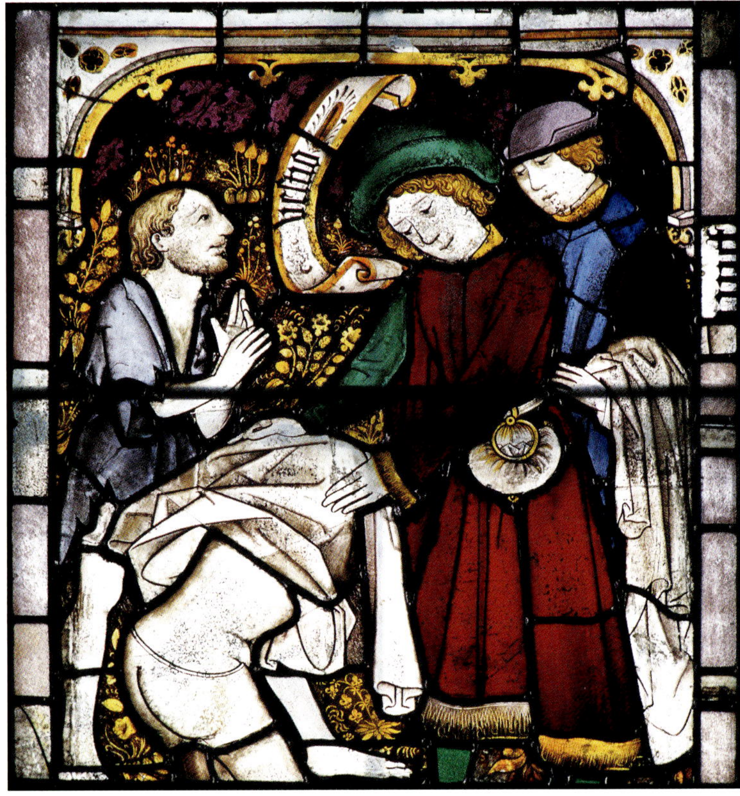

St Matthew's Gospel (25:45–6) specifically defines performance of such charitable acts in life as being an effective defence at the Last Judgement. Their resulting popularity is illustrated by numerous examples in art, ranging from wall paintings in Hărman church, Transylvania (in modern Romania), to stained glass at Tattershall church in Lincolnshire (plate 18).

## PERSONAL DEVOTION



Register of John Grandisson,
Bishop of Exeter, 1348

19
Handwritten annotation from
a book of hours; illuminated
manuscript, southern
Netherlands, 1425–49
(V&A: MSL/1902/1691, f.134r)

Alongside practical good works, it was important to maximize one's spiritual well-being. Regular confession was key, and outstanding penance that had not been completed in life would add to the time spent in Purgatory after death. The increased popularity from the thirteenth century of private prayer and meditation, alongside public worship in church, has been associated with the foundation of the Franciscan and Dominican orders, as well as with more effective pastoral work by the clergy in general. But the increasing impact of the doctrine of Purgatory may also have played its part in this changing practice, with individuals pushed to take increasing responsibility for their own spiritual welfare. A handwritten annotation in a book of hours (plate 19) lists Masses to be said and alms to be given on each day of the week, beginning:

> If a man or woman these masses underwritten do sing for himself or for any other of his friends, in what need or tribulation or sickness that they be in, they shall be delivered by the grace of god, without doubt within 10 days.

The trend was certainly assisted by the production of numerous devotional aids, many of which could also be treasured artworks. All over Europe, small-scale, delicate items appeared on the market that could confer spiritual benefit on the user, while simultaneously being a pleasure to own. A tiny English triptych (plate 20), just under 7 cm high and richly enamelled on both sides, shows scenes from the Passion and Resurrection of Christ. Its owner would have been encouraged by texts like the Franciscan *Meditations on the Life of Christ* (originally written in about 1300) to use the triptych to visualize the events as if he or she were actually present.

Many of these devotional objects featured images of Christ, the Virgin or saints – it was hoped that these would act as intercessors to plead for the welfare of one's soul after death (as in plate 16). Although Christ acted as judge, he also had an intercessionary role to play, as the Redeemer. He appears on an ivory diptych alongside his mother, the Virgin, holding a book with text that reads: 'I am the Lord your God, Jesus Christ, who created you, redeemed you and will

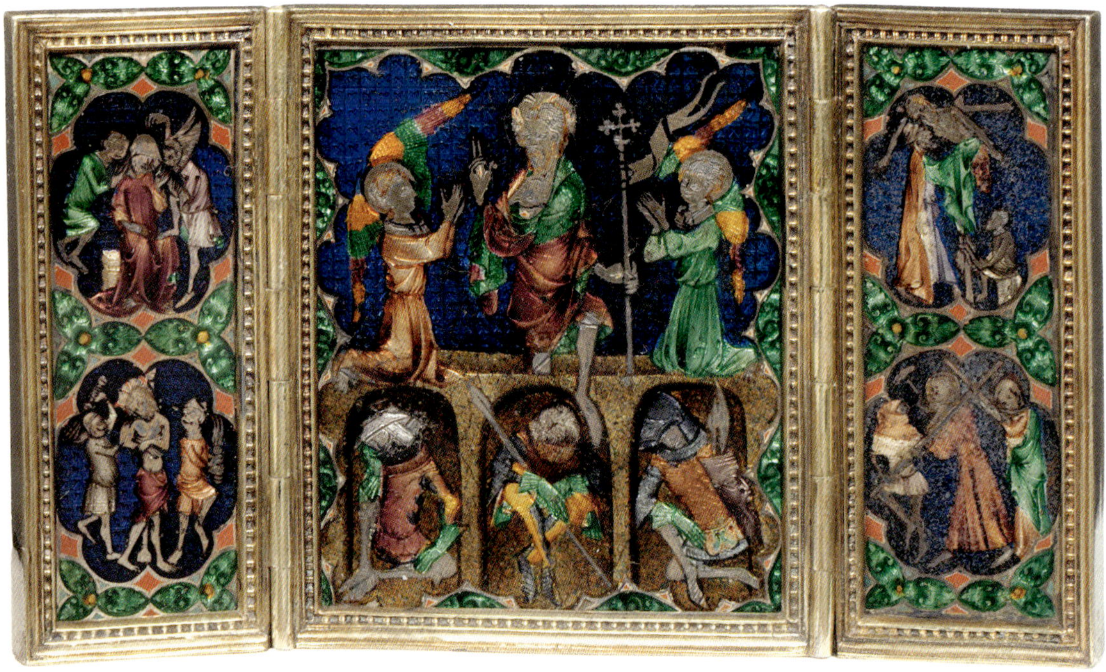

20
Triptych with scenes from the
Passion and Resurrection of
Christ; gilded silver with enamel,
England, c.1325–50
(V&A: M.545–1910)

save you' (see plate 17). The Virgin, with her unique relationship with Christ, appeared frequently as an intercessor. In an alabaster relief (plate 22) the archangel St Michael uses his scales (missing one pan) to weigh the resurrected souls at the Last Judgement, while the Virgin uses her rosary to try to save one of them. The cult of devotion to the Virgin became more and more popular from the thirteenth century onwards, largely based on her perceived powers in this important area. Images used as a focus for this devotion survive in a variety of media (for example plate 21).

Cultivating a relationship with a specific saint improved the chances of them helping one's soul after death. Books of hours – personal prayer books based on the daily monastic services that became increasingly popular from the 1200s – usually contained images of popular saints with associated prayers. These

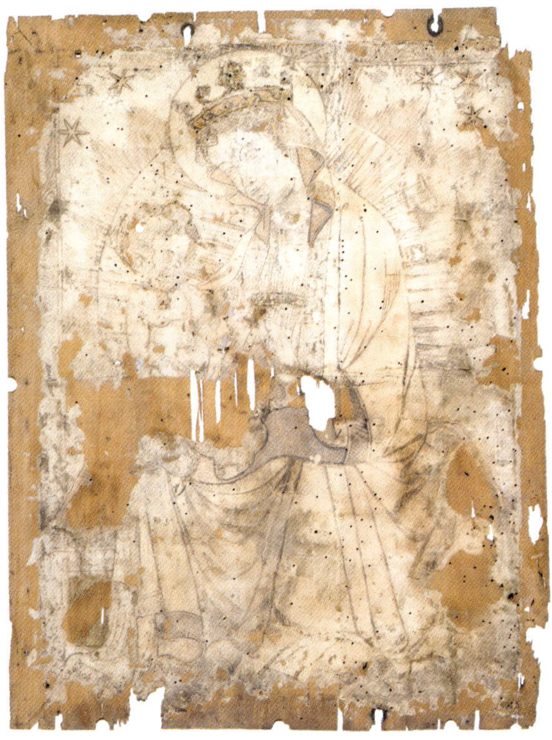

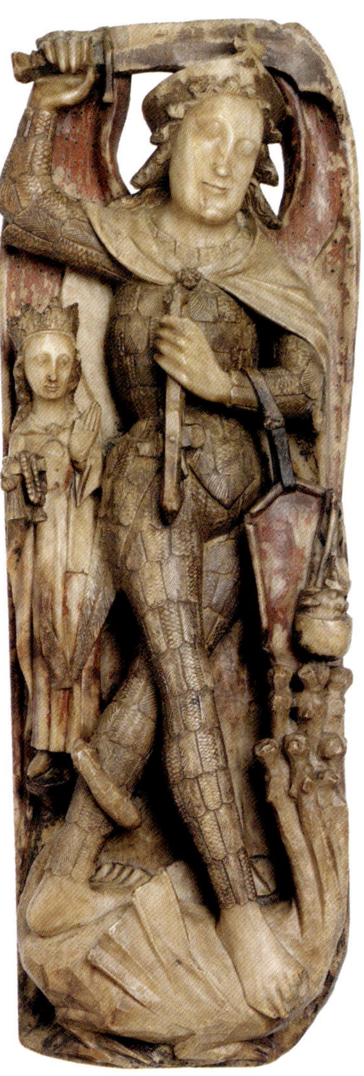

21 ABOVE
Virgin and Child; hand-coloured
woodcut on paper pasted onto
wood, northern Italy, 1450–75
(V&A, 321A–1894)

22 RIGHT
St Michael and the Virgin; alabaster
with traces of paint and gilding,
England, c.1430–70
(V&A: A.209–1946)

clearly show the influence that worshippers hoped their saints could have after
death. The prayer accompanying an image of St Barbara (plate 23) translates: 'St
Barbara, friend and succour to us, in time of necessity and in the hour of our
death. Pray for us . . . that we may be made worthy of the promises of Christ.'
Often an individual felt particularly close links with their name saint, and this is
illustrated frequently in surviving works of art. Geldulph de Nausnydere, the

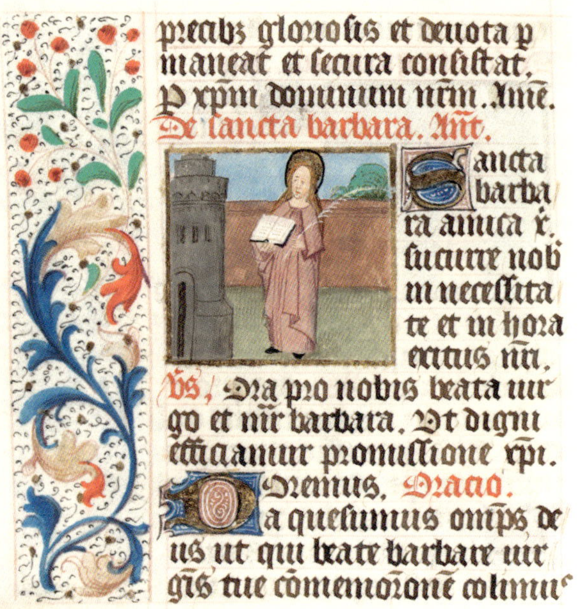

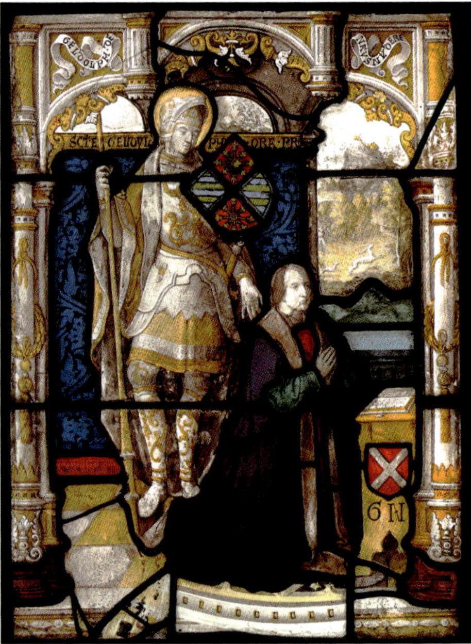

Echevin (deputy mayor) of Louvain in 1517 and 1525, is pictured with his name saint, St Geldulph (plate 24). The popular plea 'St Geldulph, pray for [me]', inscribed behind him, makes the expected intercession explicit.

CONFRATERNITIES



Confraternities flourished all over Europe, offering their members both spiritual and practical support. These organizations gave lay people the chance to safeguard the future of their souls, both directly and indirectly. In direct terms, they provided equipment for funerals and, crucially, ongoing prayers for the souls of members. Supporting a fraternity offered a communal devotional experience that enhanced the spiritual well-being that was so important in terms of preparing for death. Some confraternities had a specifically penitential function, expressed through public flagellation or whipping. A Genoese banner shows two kneeling flagellants, with the holes in their robes enabling their backs to be whipped (plate 25). Penitence was a key feature of an effective preparation for

23 OPPOSITE LEFT
St Barbara and associated prayer,
from a book of hours; illuminated
manuscript, southern Netherlands (possibly Hainault), c.1480
(V&A: MSL/1902/1674, f.85v)

24 OPPOSITE RIGHT
Geldulph de Nausnydere and
St Geldulph; stained glass,
Louvain (Netherlands), 1526
(V&A: 211–1908)

25 RIGHT
Banner of a flagellant confrater-
nity, attributed to Barnaba da
Modena; tempera and gold leaf
on canvas, Genoa (Italy), c.1370
(V&A: 781–1894)

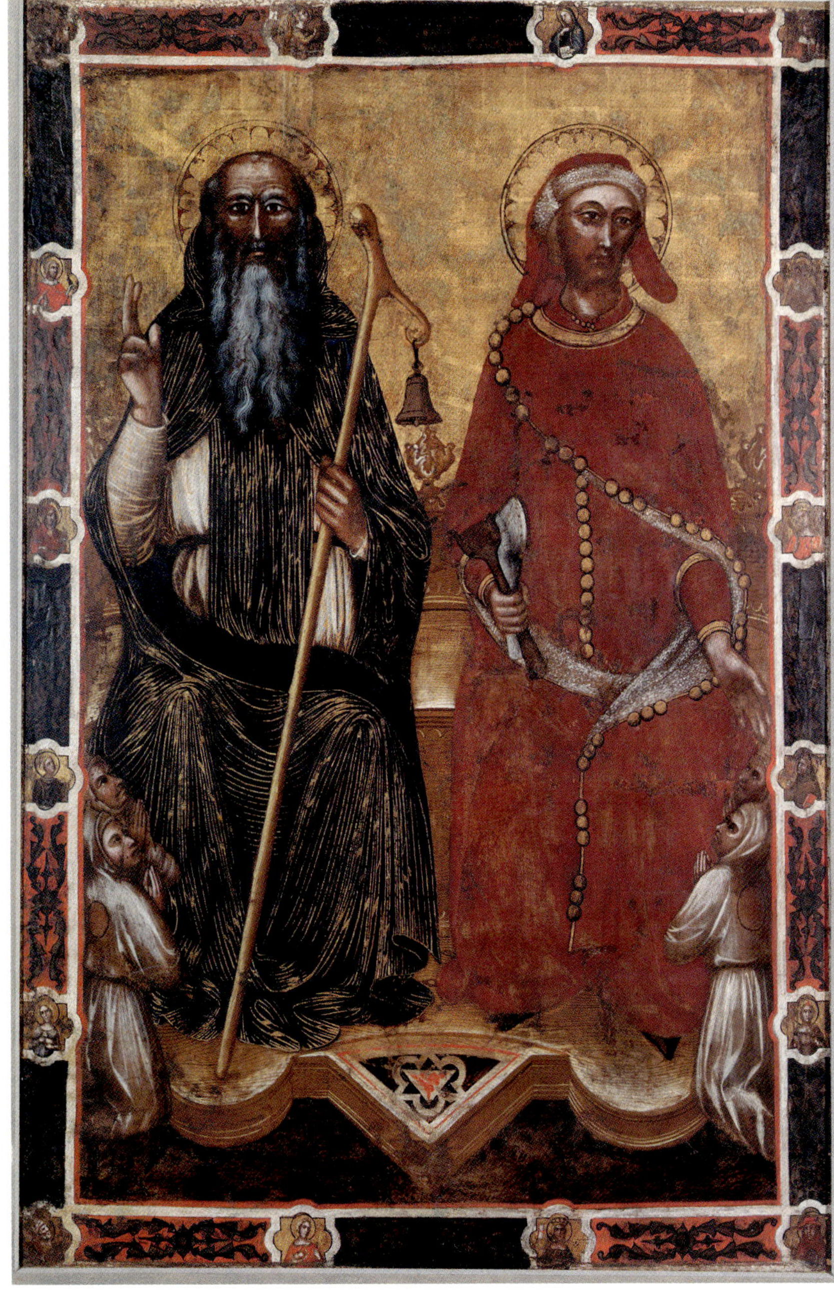

dying: purging oneself in life shortened the time to be spent doing so after death. By giving gifts to a confraternity, one expressed piety, as well as improving the chances of prayers being offered for one's soul. The Fayrey family gave a pall, embroidered with their named images (plate 26), to their confraternity of St John the Baptist in Dunstable, Bedfordshire, to be used in the funerals of its members. By this gift, the Fayreys identified themselves firmly as charitable and pious patrons.

## INDULGENCES

The development of the indulgence provided the most direct route for those seeking to shorten their time in Purgatory. Priests imposed penance in return for sins committed, and an indulgence provided a fixed period of remission from this penance. Such penance, if unfulfilled in life, translated after death into time

And we . . . have released 40 days of the penance enjoined by the gracious God on all our parishioners . . . for sins for which they are penitent, contrite and have made confession, if they pray devoutly for these things

Letter from William Zouche, Archbishop of York, to an official, 1348

26
The Fayrey funeral pall; velvet cloth-of-gold, silk velvet and silk, with metal and silk threads, England, *c.* 1516

(St Peter's church, Dunstable, Bedfordshire, on long-term loan to the V&A)

27

Reliquary of the arm bone of St
Catherine, by Raffaello Grimaldi;
gilded copper, partly gilded silver
and niello, probably Reggio-
Emilia (Italy), *c*.1482–96

(V&A: 704–1884)

in Purgatory, so in practice indulgences enabled the soul to spend less time in Purgatory. They were therefore an effective tool in influencing the behaviour of the faithful.

Popes and bishops could grant an indulgence, usually in return for a specified devotional activity, undertaken in a spirit of repentance and piety. This might include supporting the building or rebuilding of a church, going on pilgrimage to a specific place or saying particular prayers. Such attention could have important effects on church building and decoration. In 1245, Pope Innocent IV granted an indulgence to those who contributed to the rebuilding of Westminster Abbey, even though Henry III was covering most of the cost of the lavish rebuild from his own pocket. Indulgences granted by Pope Nicholas IV in 1288 for visiting Assisi, the burial place of St Francis, contributed to the cost of decorating the celebrated basilica there. The plenary indulgence (full remission from all penance) offered by Pope Boniface VIII to those who visited the basilicas of Sts Peter and Paul in Rome during the Jubilee year of 1300 led to a huge influx of pilgrims. On a smaller scale, an Italian reliquary carries an inscription offering an indulgence of 40 days for anyone who kisses it, which presumably made it a focus of attention in the cathedral at Reggio where it was housed (plate 27).

An indulgence could also be attached to a particular subject or image, increasing its popularity. Meditation on the instruments of Christ's death (the *Arma Christi*) was believed to provide remission from penance, and saying the Lord's Prayer and other specified prayers before the image rendered this devotional act even more efficacious. A typical rubric in a book of hours reads:

To them that before this image of pity devoutly say five pater noster [Lord's Prayer], five Aves [*Ave Marias*] and a Credo [the Creed] piteously beholding these arms of Christ's passion are granted 32 thousand 7 hundred and 55 years of pardon.

28
Rosary; wood, silver, gilded silver and
amber, Germany, *c*.1475–1500
(V&A: 517–1903)

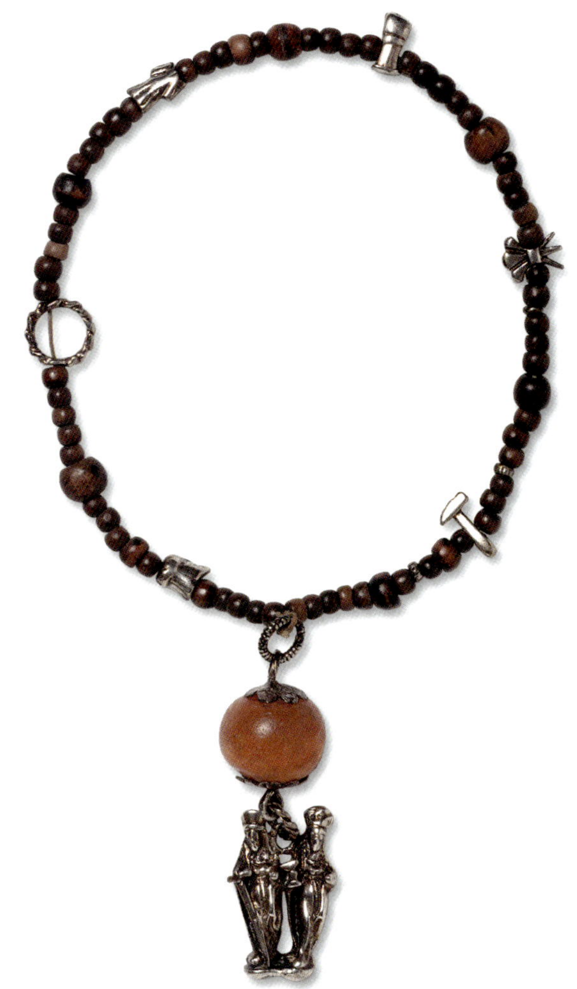

The design of a German rosary has been influenced by this common devotional
practice (plate 28). The small wooden beads each represent an *Ave* and the larger
ones *Pater Nosters*. In between are silver representations of the *Arma Christi*.
Indulgences were not intended to encourage mechanical repetition of prayers: a
devotional booklet (plate 29) incorporates images of the *Arma Christi* set
amongst narrative images of Christ's death. It would have encouraged the owner
(probably the monk pictured on the ivory front) to set his meditation on the
Instruments of Christ's Passion in the emotive context of the actual events.

29
Devotional booklet; ivory, paint and gold leaf, possibly Lower Rhine (Germany), 1330–50
(V&A: 11–1872)

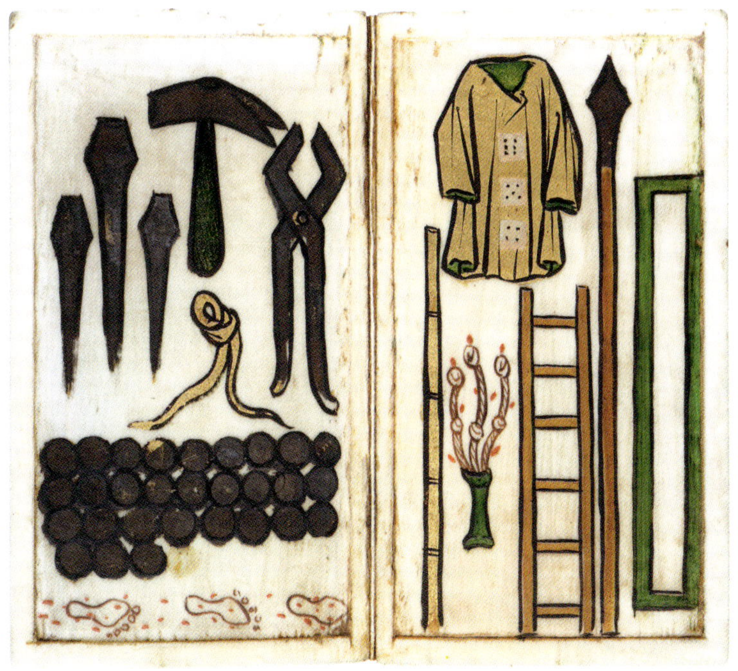

## PATRONAGE

Remember the Lady Isabelle Despenser, Countess of Warwick, who founded this chapel . . . May God have pity on her soul. Amen

Translation of a Latin inscription on the Despenser Chapel, Tewkesbury Abbey, Gloucestershire, 1422–38

Gifts that beautified the worship of God provided a permanent demonstration of an individual's devotion and charity, which would be counted in their favour at the Last Judgement. It was also important to keep one's name constantly in the memory of others as a pious and deserving donor, and thus encourage their prayers after one's death. In England, parishes kept bede rolls listing the names of the dead. These were recited at annual services of remembrance, or obits, and other occasions to solicit prayers for their souls. It was relatively inexpensive to put one's name on this roll, but a specific gift to the church – such as a candle, vestment or other church ornament – would merit a special mention. Giles

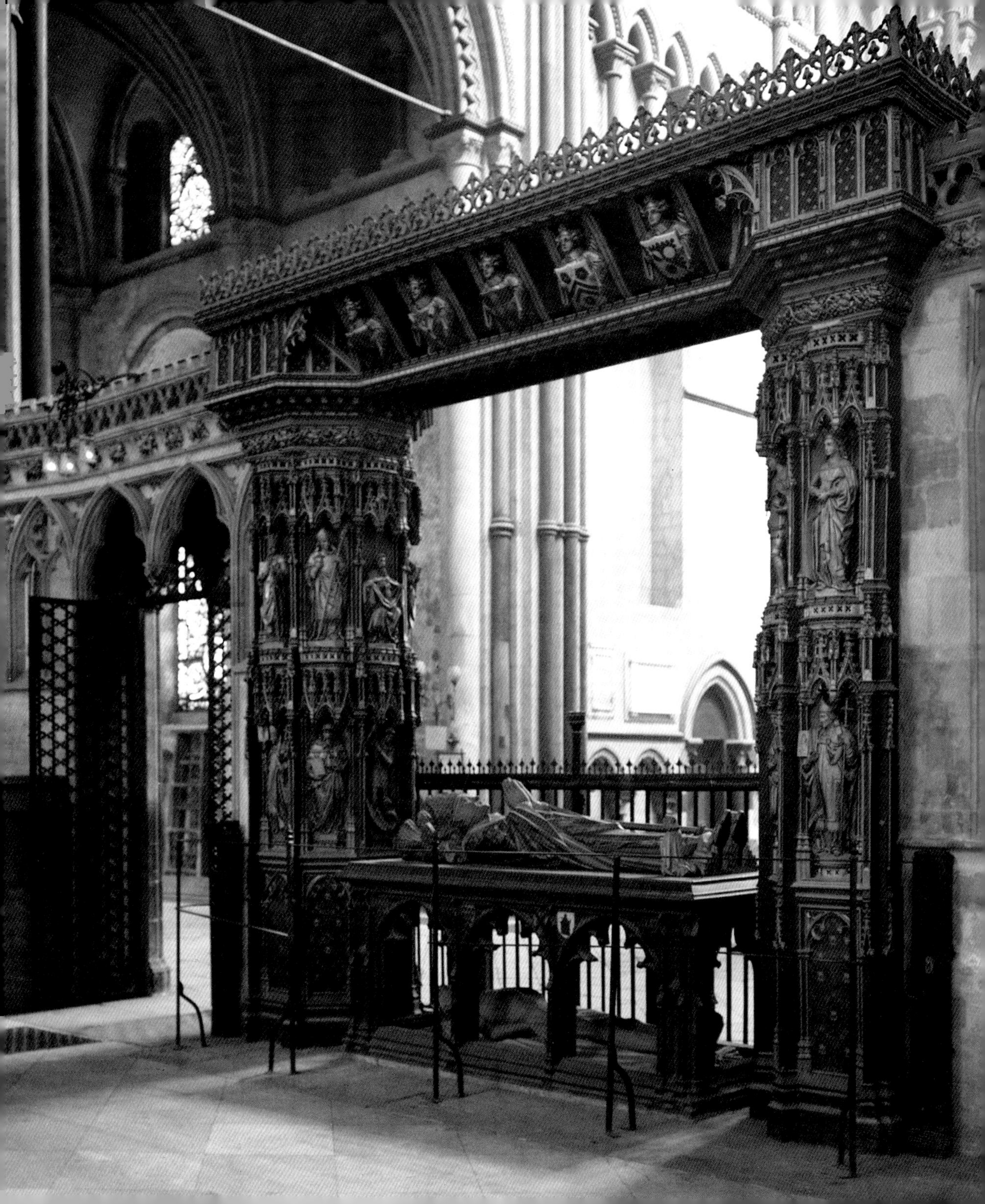

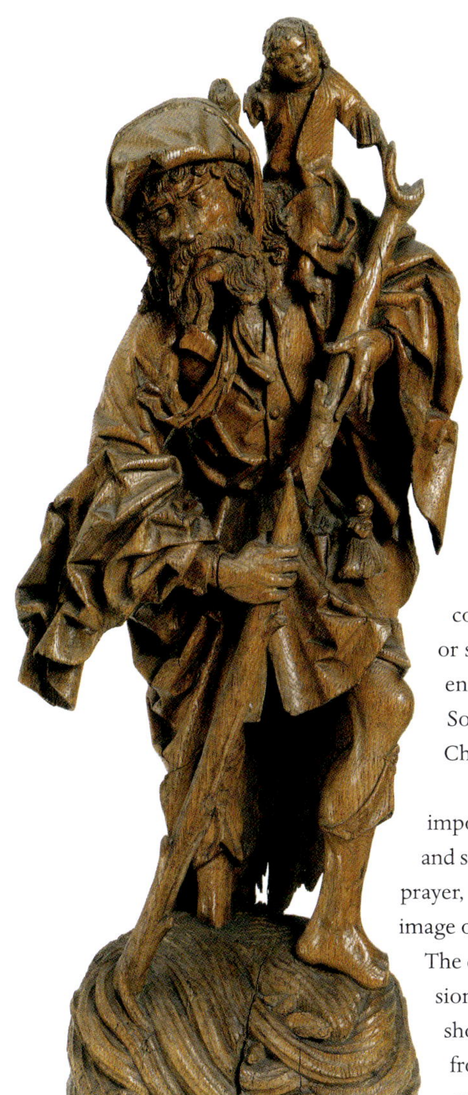


Tomb of Archbishop Chichele, effigies possibly by John Massingham, tomb probably by Thomas Mapilton; stone, England, complete by 1426
(Canterbury Cathedral, Kent)

The upper effigy shows the archbishop in his full vestments while below another, of his cadaver, can be glimpsed within the tomb chest.

31 LEFT
St Christopher with donor, Master of Elsloo; oak, Limburg (Netherlands), c.1520
(V&A: 374–1890)

Palmer of Hoo St Mary's, Kent, bequeathed money for a vestment 'to the intent to have my soul there specially in the bede roll prayed for'. On a larger scale, the wealthiest donors could found a college or other charitable institution, such as a hospital, almshouse or school. Here prayers for founders would be enshrined in statutes, ensuring remembrance in perpetuity. Even today, the college of All Souls, Oxford, maintains the tomb of its founder, Archbishop Chichele (1362–1441), at Canterbury Cathedral (plate 30).

It is clear from surviving artefacts that identifying the donor was important. Images of donors appear in all media, from prayer books and sculpture to stained glass and paintings. Usually they are kneeling in prayer, but sometimes they are included more ingeniously. In a devotional image of St Christopher, the donor is carried in the saint's purse (plate 31). The donor could be further identified by an inscription, or by the inclusion of a coat of arms or a merchant's mark. A stained-glass panel showing Abbot Heinrich von Binsfeld of Cornelimünster, originally from Mariawald Abbey, Cologne, featured both a coat of arms and an inscription, so that there could be no mistake (plate 32). Presenting the donor in visual form encouraged prayers for his or her soul.

32 RIGHT
Abbot Heinrich von Binsfeld of
Corneliimünster; stained glass,
Lower Rhine (Germany), c.1520–26
(V&A: C.323–1928)

33 OPPOSITE
Chasuble with the arms of Sir Thomas
Erpingham; silk and linen, with metal
and silk threads, Italian silk with
English embroidery, c.1400–30
(V&A: T.256–1967)

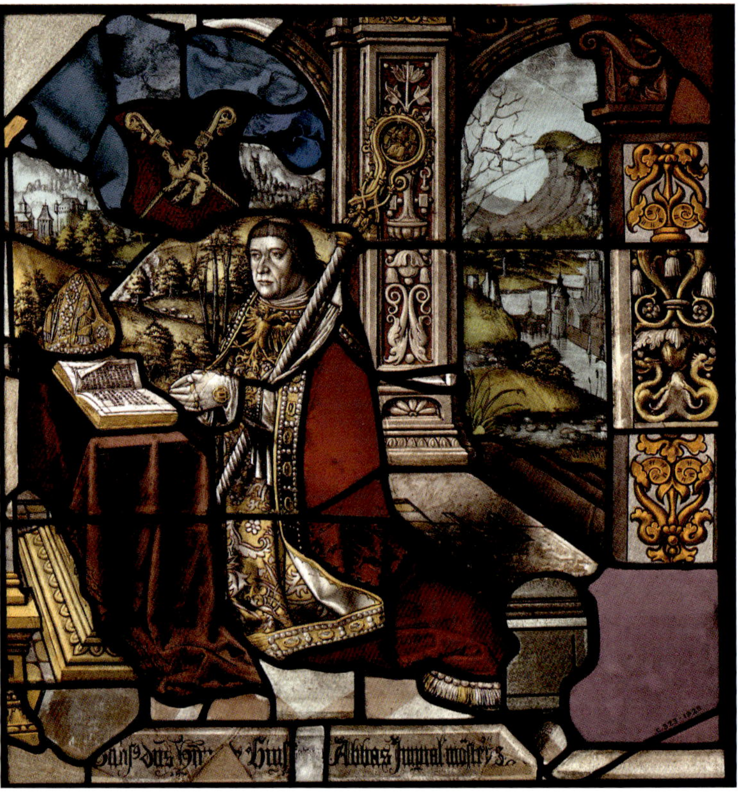

Some forms of patronage enabled donors to include their names directly
in parish liturgy. By commissioning a vestment bearing their image or arms to
be worn by the officiating priest, they could ensure the attention of the parish
every time Mass was celebrated. An early fifteenth-century chasuble (plate 33)
has the arms of Sir Thomas Erpingham on the back: these would have remained
clearly visible to the congregation throughout the ritual. This interest in recog-
nition was not simply a cynical exercise in self-promotion. Donor images,
inscriptions and arms also appear on private devotional objects, particularly

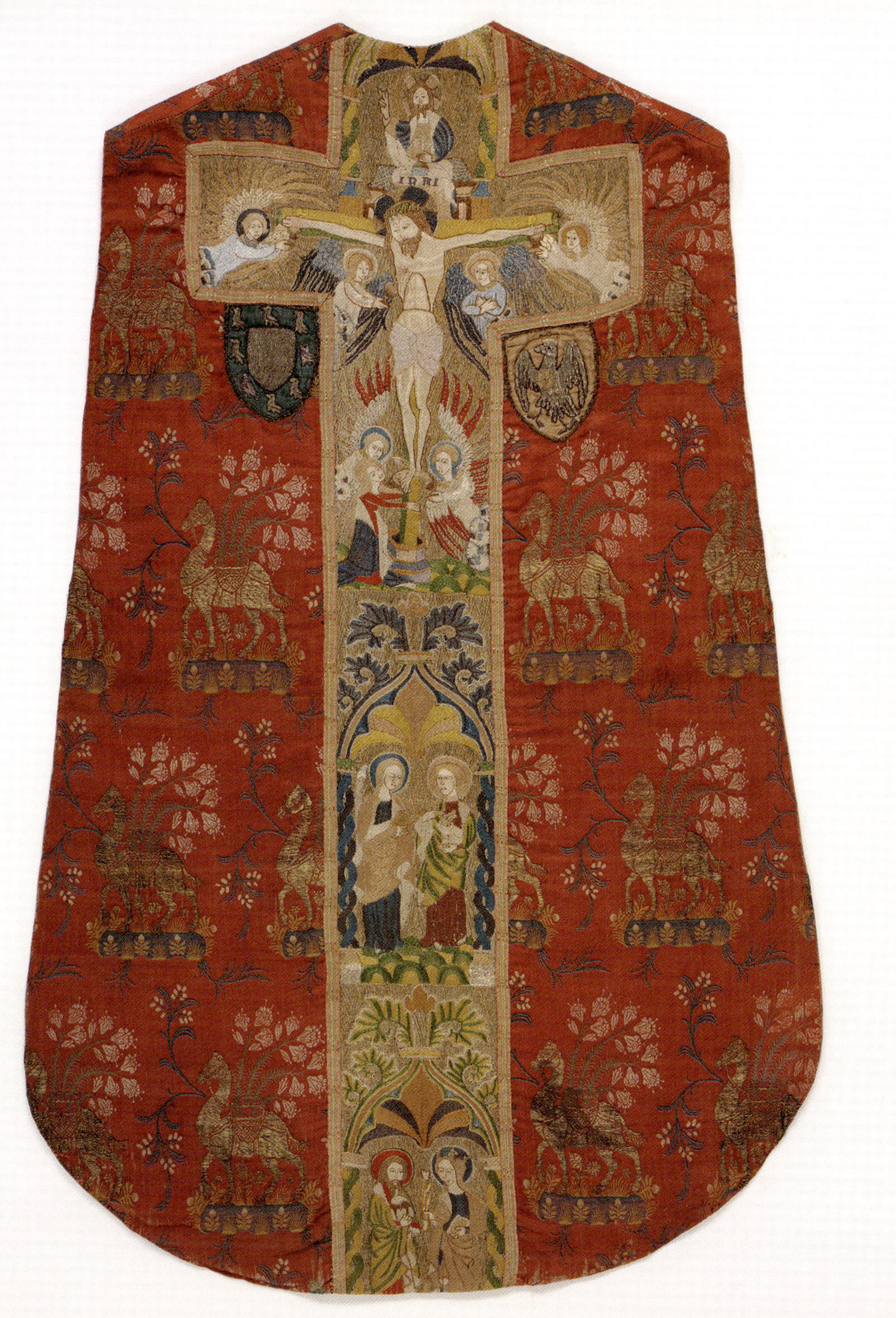

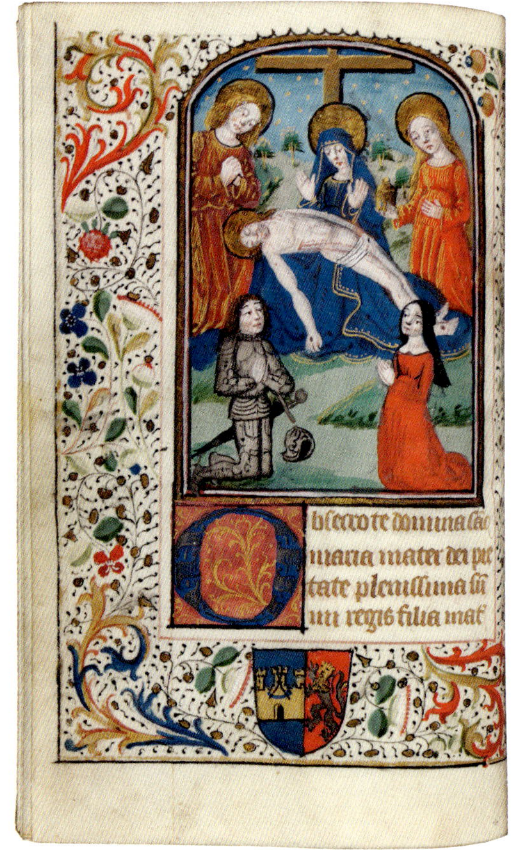

prayer books (plate 34). This was thought to reinforce the donor's personal piety in the eyes of God and the saints that might act as intercessors (here the Virgin and Sts John the Evangelist and Mary Magdalene), in the hope that this would help them after death.



MEMENTO MORI

Everyone was encouraged to make similar preparations by the popularity of *memento mori* images. Intended to remind the viewer of his or her own mortality, and thus encourage preparation for death while there was still time, these

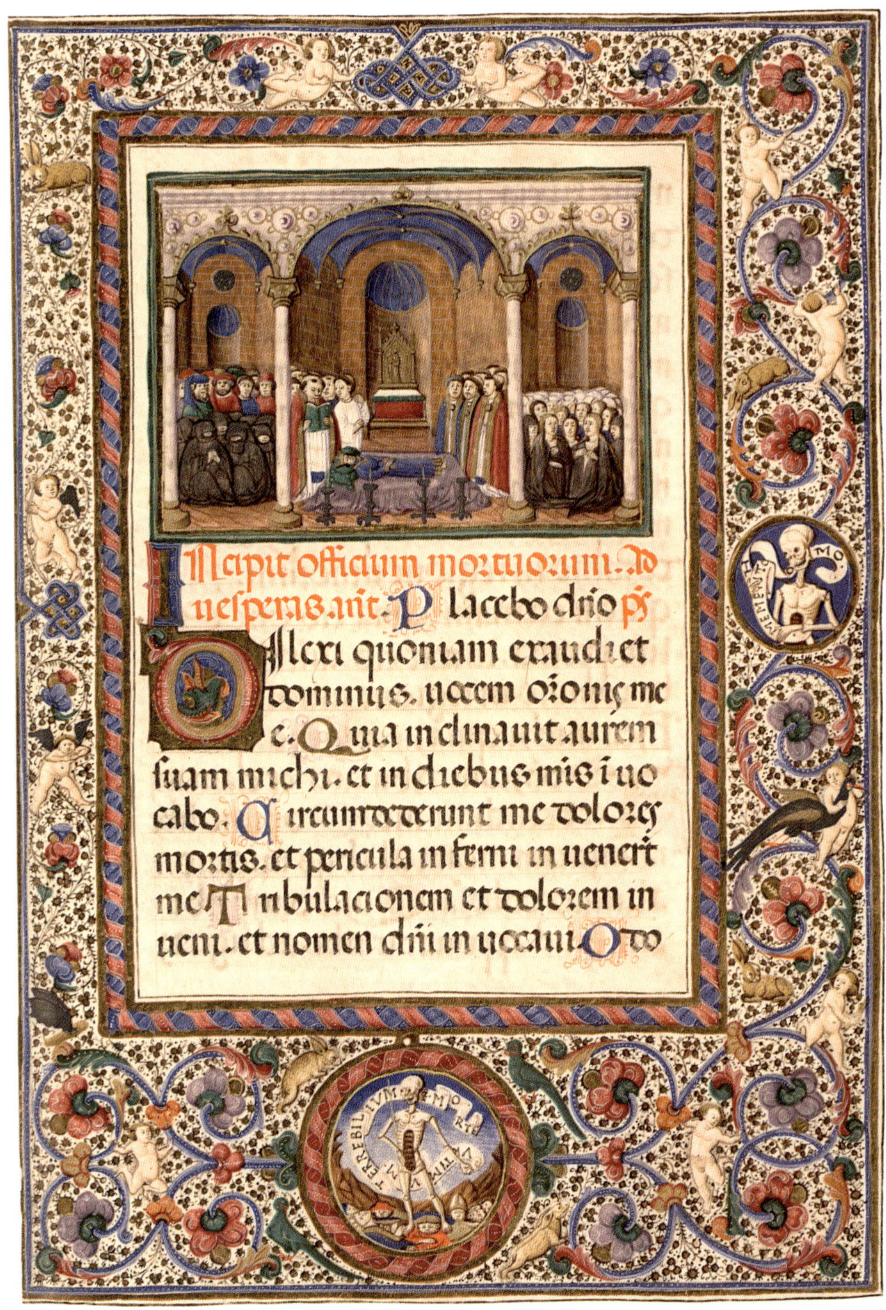
Incipit officium mortuorum. Ad
uesperas ant. Placebo dño ps
Dilexi quoniam exaudiet
dominus. uocem orationis me
e. Quia inclinauit aurem
suam michi. et in diebus meis i uo
cabo. Circumdederunt me dolores
mortis. et pericula inferni inuene
me Tribulacionem et dolorem in
ueni. et nomen dñi inuocaui O do

36 RIGHT
Pendant with *memento mori*;
rock crystal, France, 1450–1500
(V&A: A.48–1935)

37 OPPOSITE
The Three Living and the Three
Dead from the Serristori Hours;
illuminated manuscript,
Florence (Italy), *c.*1500
(V&A: MSL/1921/1722, f.57v)

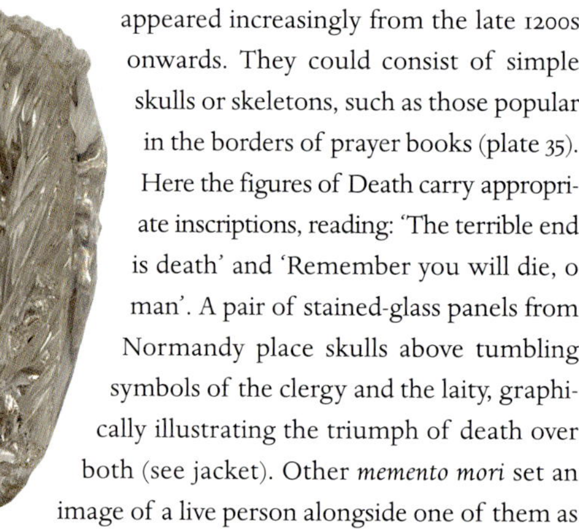

appeared increasingly from the late 1200s onwards. They could consist of simple skulls or skeletons, such as those popular in the borders of prayer books (plate 35). Here the figures of Death carry appropriate inscriptions, reading: 'The terrible end is death' and 'Remember you will die, o man'. A pair of stained-glass panels from Normandy place skulls above tumbling symbols of the clergy and the laity, graphically illustrating the triumph of death over both (see jacket). Other *memento mori* set an image of a live person alongside one of them as dead. A rock-crystal pendant shows the face of a young woman on one side and a skull on the other (plate 36); the girl's head can be seen reflected in the eye sockets of the skull.

This juxtaposition of the living and the dead is illustrated forcefully in the popular subject of the Three Living and Three Dead. This probably originated in a late thirteenth-century French poem, which describes how three men went out hunting and came across three corpses who lectured them on their worldly ways, closing with the chilling words: 'as you are, we once were; as we are, so shall you be'. This imagery spread rapidly across Europe, even to Italy (plate 37) where scenes of the macabre were not generally as popular, and was widely circulated through woodcuts. A French book of hours displays a variant on the theme: the figure of Death shows a richly dressed young man an image of himself as a corpse, as his soul (represented as a tiny naked figure) leaves his body (plate 38).

The *Danse Macabre*, or Dance of Death, also confronted living individuals with their dead selves, as they danced with their own corpses. It seems to have appeared first in visual form in wall paintings around the cloisters of the cemetery of Les Innocents, Paris (1424–5). Again taken up by printers, the image was circulated widely across Europe. The border scenes in a French book of hours continue for 12 consecutive openings, showing people from the top of society

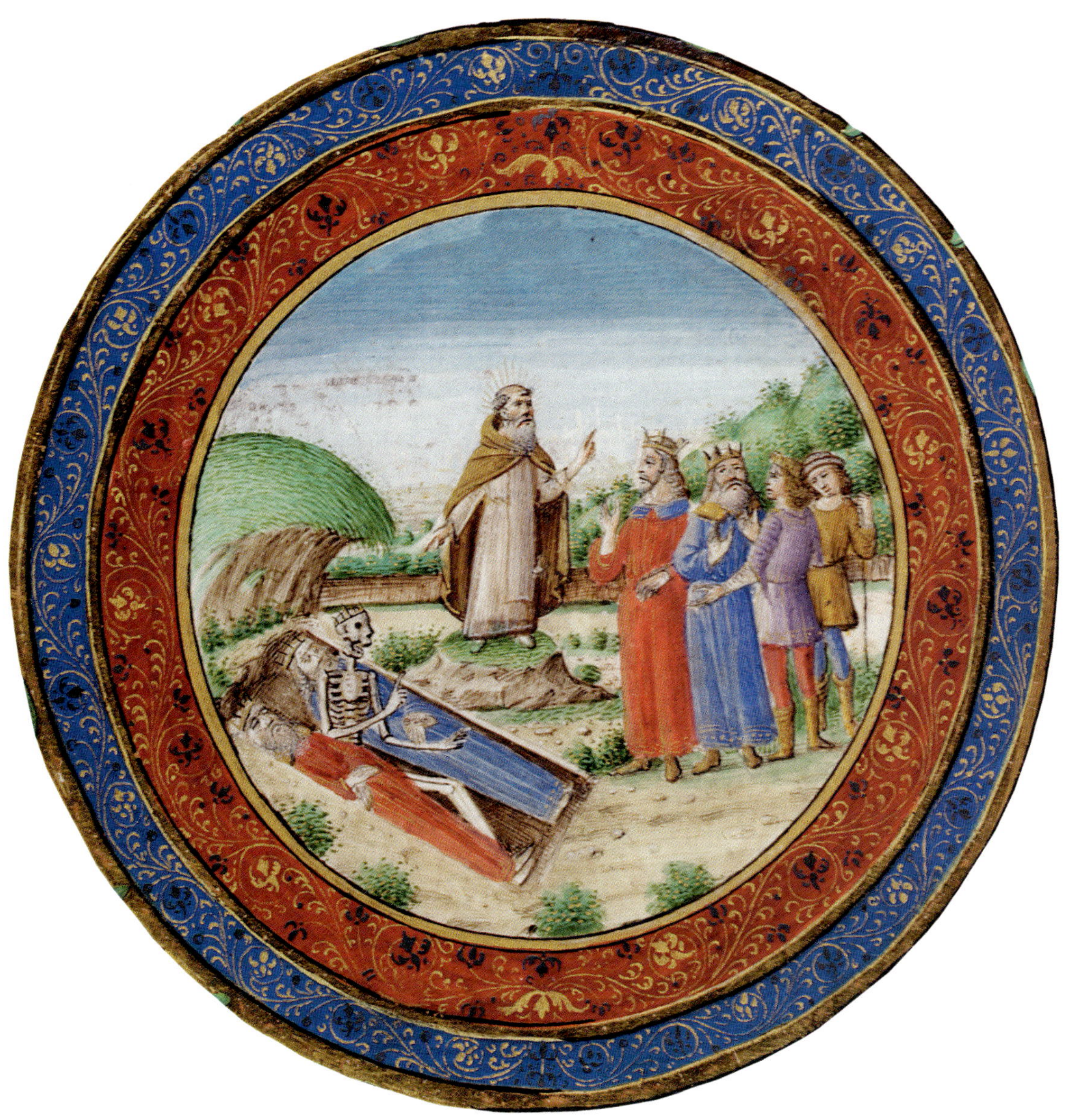

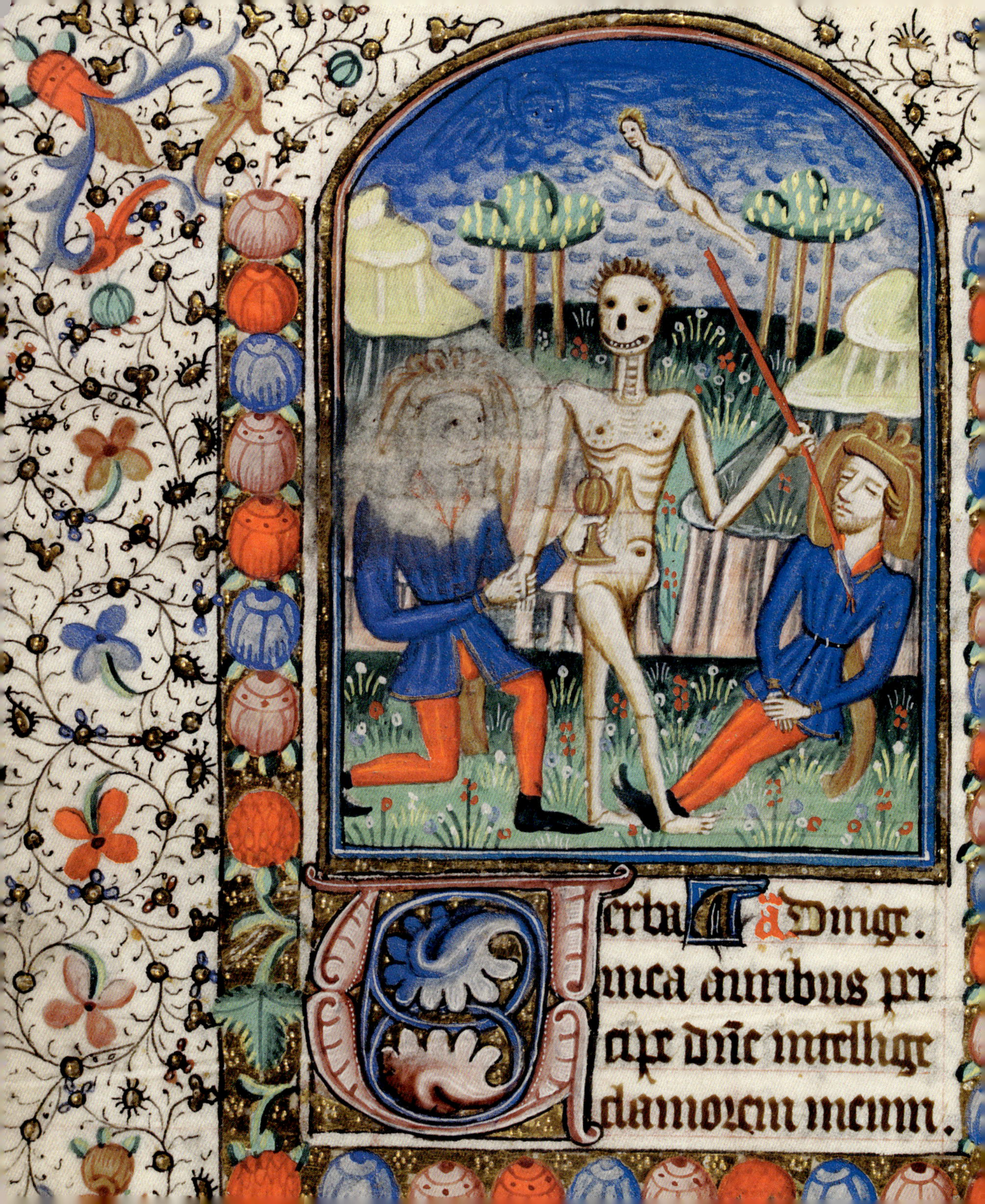
Verba ¶ A. Dirige.
mea auribus pr
ape dñe intellige
clamorem meum.

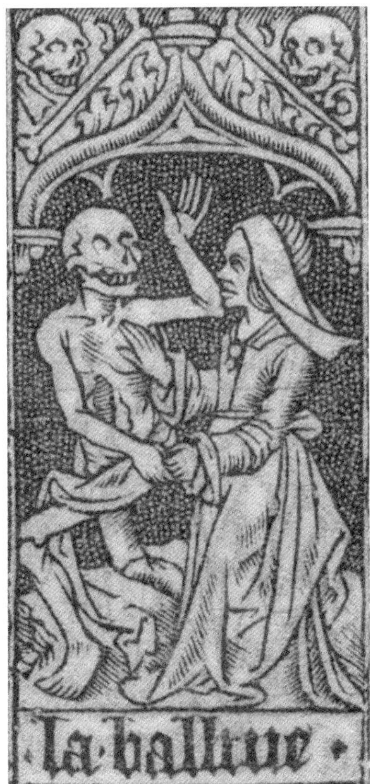
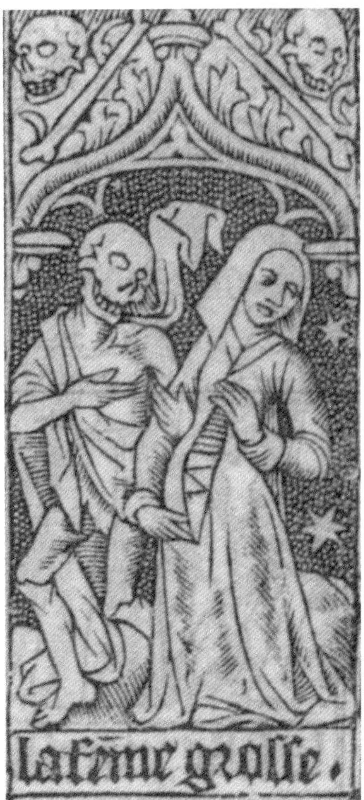

38 OPPOSITE
Death shows a living man his corpse, from a book of hours; illuminated manuscript, France (Paris or Bayeux), *c.*1450
(V&A: MSL/1902/1650, f.98v)

39 RIGHT
Scenes showing the Dance of Death, from a book of hours; printed by Philippe Pigouchet, Paris (France), ?1501
(38041800152019, ff.gv verso and gvi)

downwards: from kings and popes through clerics, fat ladies and children to labourers, each specified with an inscription (plate 39). They are all accompanied by an image of themselves as a cadaver. The message is clear: death is the one certainty for everyone, whatever their status.

The popularity of *memento mori* has been associated with the terrors of the Black Death, but interest in the inescapable nature of death dates from well before 1348. It combined the natural anxiety felt over the uncertain future faced by the soul after death with a reminder to do whatever one could about it. This was the dual concern that underlay much of the artistic production during this period.

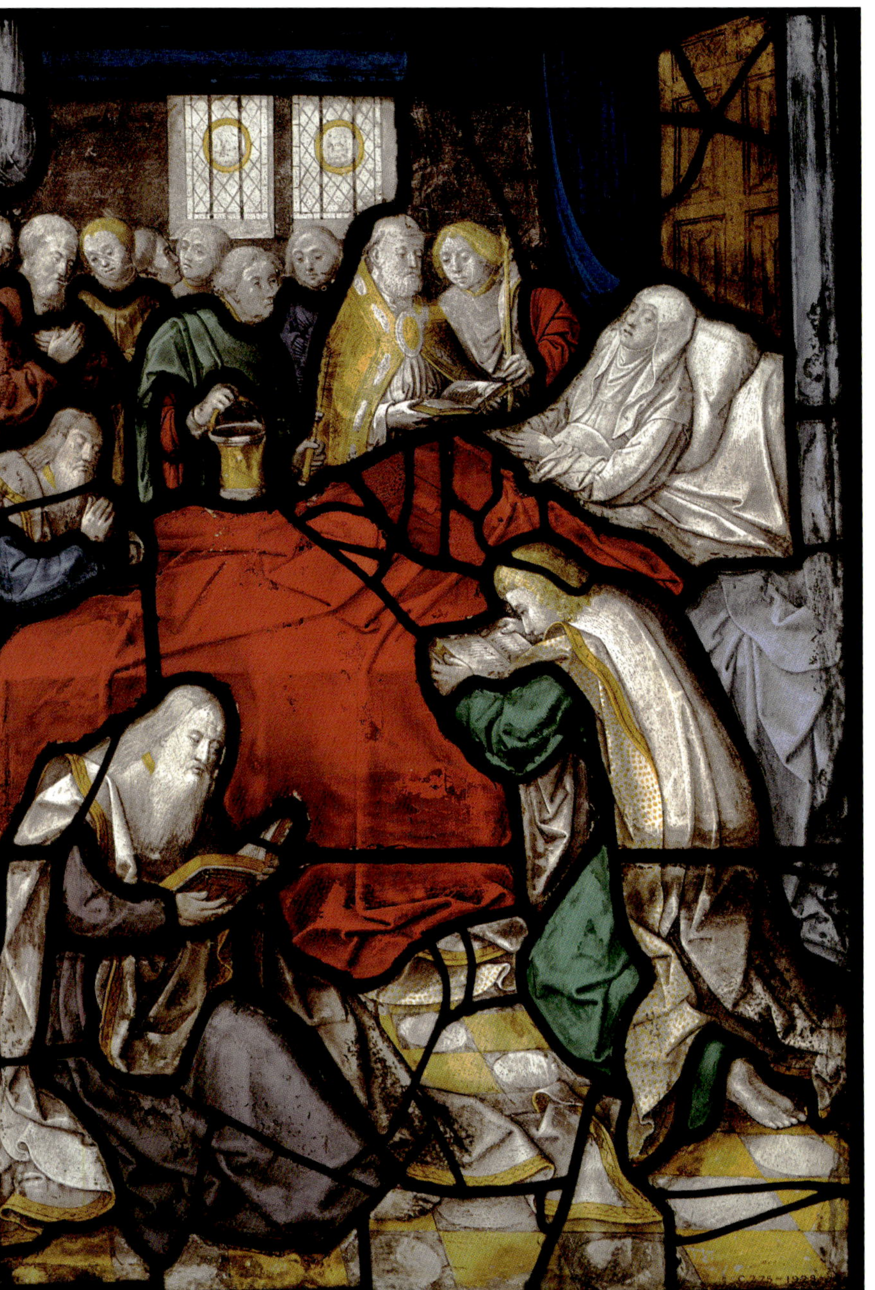

# CHAPTER 3

# Dying well

The way in which a person died and was buried was believed to have a direct effect on the subsequent fate of their soul. One of the particular horrors of the recurring outbreaks of plague, in 1348/9 and afterwards, was their chaotic effect on the rituals of dying. Victims were sometimes overcome very suddenly, with priests unavailable or too frightened to offer the essential deathbed services. Bodies, multiplying rapidly, were flung into mass graves without the approved ceremonies.

Dying suddenly without the essential preparation provided by a priest was a particular horror, feared right across Europe. It could mean an extended spell in Purgatory, or even being consigned to Hell without hope of redemption. The Virgin and specific saints were believed to offer protection against sudden death. The *Obsecro Te* ('I beseech thee') prayer, a popular feature of books of hours, was often accompanied by an image of the Pietà (Virgin with the dead Christ) (plate 34). It asked her to reveal the expected time of death, and was sometimes accompanied by a reassuring rubric: 'To all them that . . . daily say devoutly this prayer before our blessed Lady of Pity, she will . . . warn them the day [and] the hour of death.'

Seeing, and praying to, an image of St Christopher protected one from sudden death on that particular day, and consequently the saint appeared in wall paintings from England to Slovenia, often placed directly opposite the church door for the benefit of the passer-by glancing in (plate 41). A Norman-French inscription that accompanies the fourteenth-century St Christopher in Wood-eaton church, Oxfordshire, spells this out: 'Who sees this image shall not die an ill [that is, sudden] death this day.' Unsurprisingly, devotional images of the saint were also popular (plate 42). St Barbara possessed similar protective powers, which were mentioned in prayers: 'Grant O Lord, through the intercession of St Barbara, that before we die we receive the sacrament of the Body and Blood of Our Lord.' It made sense to carry these saints' protection with you at all times, hence their frequent appearances on devotional jewellery (plate 43).

40 OPPOSITE
Death of the Virgin; stained glass, Brabant (Netherlands), *c.*1530
(V&A: C.275–1928)

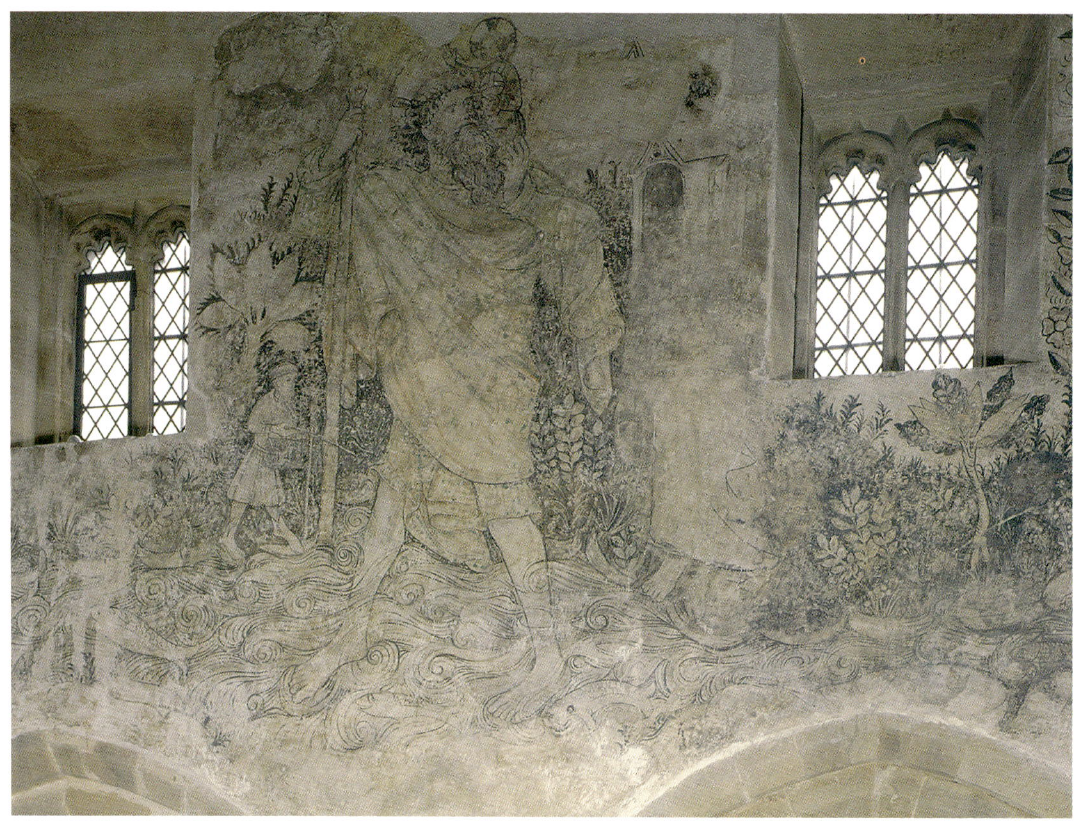





Preparation for death began with an emphasis on resolving worldly issues. Thomas Kebell's will of 1500 is typical: 'I heartily beg my executors to satisfy and truly pay my debts to everyone to whom I am indebted; also I beg them to recompense all those people to whom I have done any harm in any way.' Any unfinished business risked incurring extra penance in Purgatory. Wills, often made at the last moment, usually combined such temporal concerns with the familiar efforts to save the maker's soul, perhaps by providing revenues or adornment for a favoured church.

When Robert Gylmyn, of Seasalter near Whitstable, Kent, died in 1498, he left one shilling to have within 'a competent time after my decease . . . a stone

41 OPPOSITE
St Christopher; wall painting,
Derbyshire (England), *c.*1427
(Haddon Hall Chapel, Derbyshire)

42 RIGHT
St Christopher; alabaster, England,
*c.*1450
(V&A: A.18–1921)

43 FAR RIGHT
Ring with Sts Barbara and Christopher;
engraved gold, England, 15th century
(V&A: 690–1871)

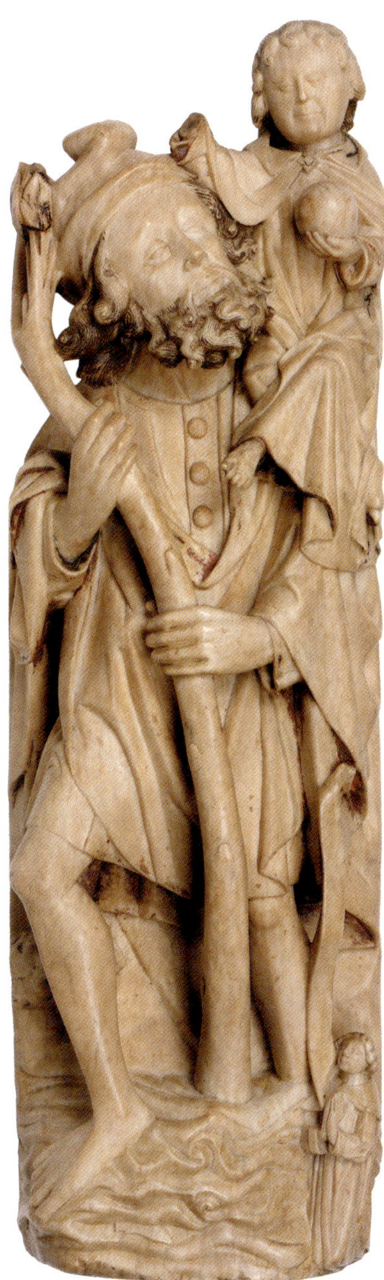

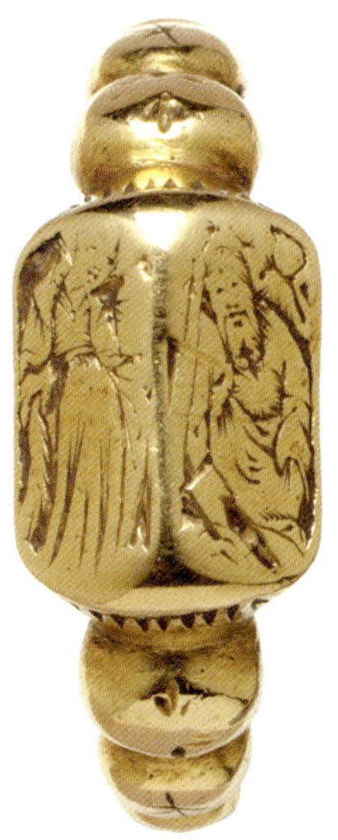

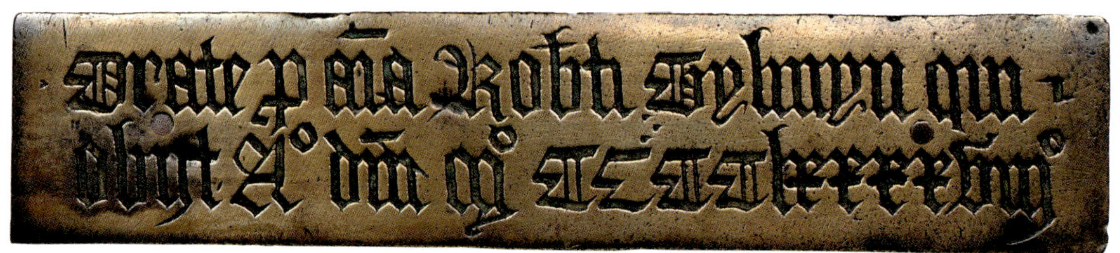

44 ABOVE
Plaque with inscription to the
memory of Robert Gylmyn;
brass, England, 1498
(V&A: M.5–1943)

45 RIGHT
The moment of death, from the
*Ars Moriendi*; printed by Johann
Weyssenburger, Nuremberg
(Germany), 1510–11
(V&A: L.366–1880, f.c.iii v)

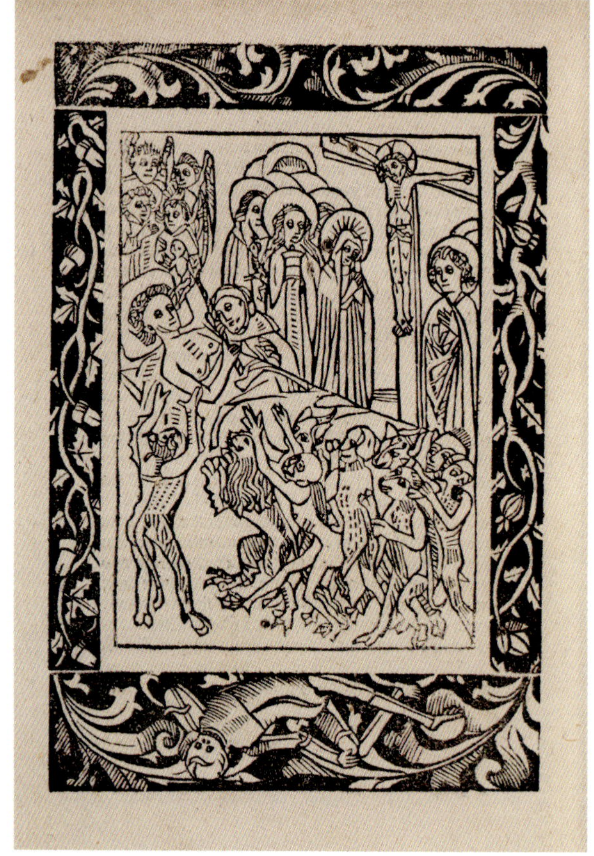

6 feet by 2 feet 6 inches wide to lie on me in the Church: Robt Gillmyn 1498'. A plaque (plate 44), with its engraved inscription, is all that remains of the monumental brass set into his tombstone. The will also provided for repairs to the 'body of the church where most needed' and for candles to an image of Our Lady of Hokday, as well as for new torches for his burial, alms to the poor on the day of the funeral, memorial Masses, the repair of a local road and the maintenance of a local shrine to Our Lady of Borstall.

The way in which a person died was crucial for the fate of his or her soul. A new genre of literature describing the ideal death swept across Europe. The *Ars Moriendi* (or Art of Dying) was originally an elaborated version of the order of service used by clergy when visiting the sick. It sets out appropriate preparations, describing the sort of death that maximizes a soul's chances of salvation. The full text first appeared in 1415 and was subsequently translated into most western European languages and circulated in printed form. From the later fif-

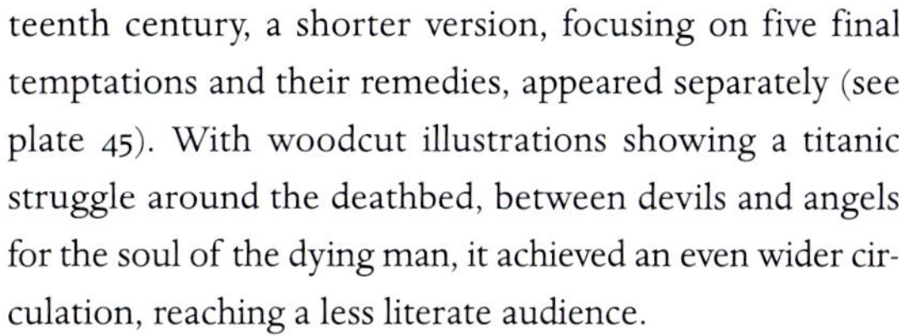

teenth century, a shorter version, focusing on five final temptations and their remedies, appeared separately (see plate 45). With woodcut illustrations showing a titanic struggle around the deathbed, between devils and angels for the soul of the dying man, it achieved an even wider circulation, reaching a less literate audience.

The ideal death was also represented in images of the deaths of saints, and in particular of the Virgin (for example, see plate 40). The attendance of a priest was essential: in that image we can see St Peter reading the Last Rites to the dying Virgin, surrounded by devout apostles who pray and read appropriate texts. Another apostle holds a bucket for holy water, with a sprinkler. The sprinkling of holy water was recommended by the *Ars Moriendi* 'that fiends may be voided from them [the dying]'. Another version of the scene (plate 46) shows one apostle helping the dying Virgin hold a candle, while another holds a censer below. This would have scented the air, enhancing the sanctity of the occasion.

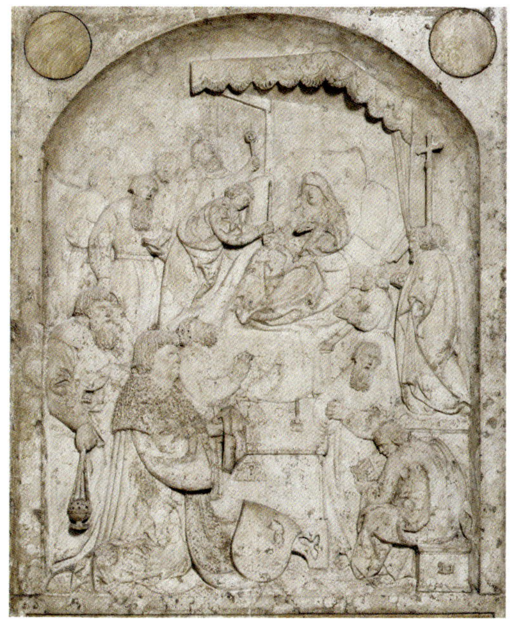

46
Death of the Virgin; stone, workshop of Loy Hering, Eichstätt (Germany), *c.*1530–40
(V&A: 4571–1859)

47
St Catherine; painted terracotta,
Utrecht (Netherlands), *c.*1480
(V&A: 7703–1861)

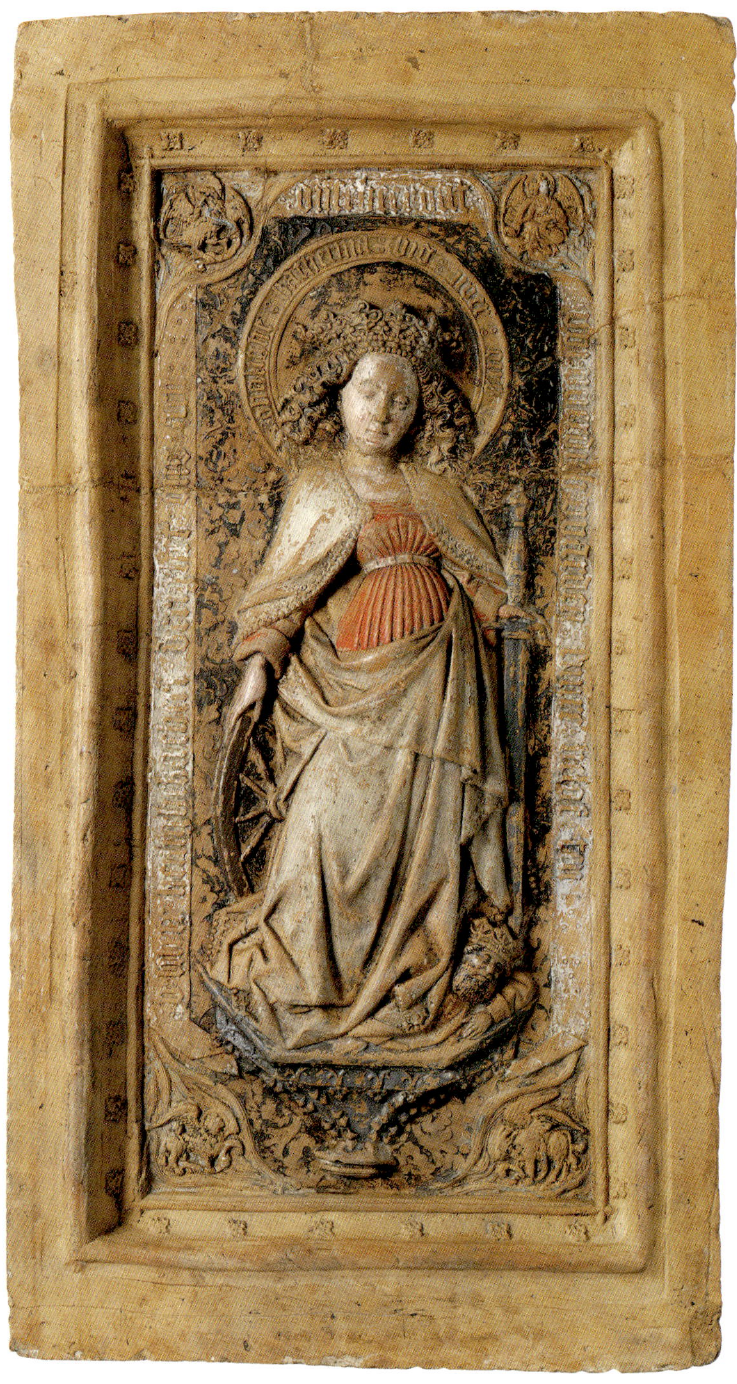

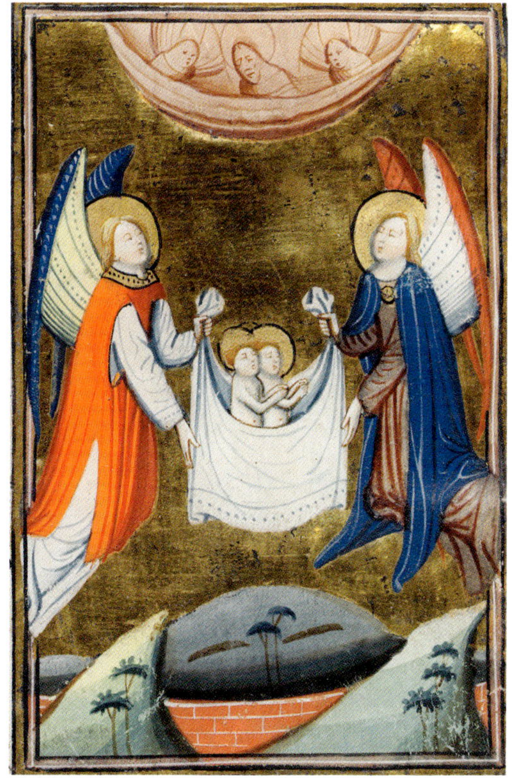

48

Angels taking souls to Heaven in
a napkin, from a book of hours;
illuminated manuscript, Netherlands,
*c.*1440

(V&A: MSL/1902/1690, f.82v)

Ideally the person dying was made aware of the approach of death and was able to participate in the Last Rites. It was best to be surrounded by devout family and friends, to pray, chant psalms and litanies and act as witnesses. The Last Rites consisted of three elements. First, the priest was expected to question the dying person about their sins in confession, before providing absolution – even last-minute repentance could save the soul from the eternal tortures of Hell. Confession was followed by the Communion, or *Viaticum*, literally a meal to sustain the soul for the journey ahead. Finally the priest anointed the dying person with holy oil in the act of Extreme Unction. Although this was essential to send the soul safely on its way, anointing was much feared, as the ultimate 'last thing'. There was no going back from this point, and it was popularly believed that those who survived afterwards could only lead a half-life, being forbidden for example from sexual activity with their spouse, as well as from eating meat.

Certain saints were particularly favoured on the deathbed, as powerful intercessors for the soul as it entered the afterlife. These included the Virgin, Sts John the Baptist and Evangelist and St Michael, familiar figures from Last Judgement scenes. The powers of St Catherine were acknowledged in images used for private devotion (for example plate 47). In the popular *Golden Legend*, she is described praying at her execution that anyone 'who invokes me at the moment of death . . . may receive the benefit of your kindness'. The example shown opposite has an inscription: 'O sweet Saint Catherine, introduce us to Our Lord, fulfilling therefore thy promises.'

After death, the Commendation of Souls was said, committing the soul to the care of the angels. The refrain 'May Christ who called thee receive thee, and may the angels lead thee to Abraham's bosom' is often accompanied in books of hours by an image of angels carefully carrying a soul (or souls) in a napkin (plate 48). The body was then prepared for burial.

## FUNERAL RITES



Introduction to Giovanni Boccaccio's
*The Decameron*, early 1350s

49
Plate showing Pope Leo X in procession
to Florence; tin-glazed earthenware,
Montelupo (Italy), *c.* 1516
(V&A: 8928–1863)

Although the details of funeral practice vary in different countries, and between different classes, the liturgy – and thus the overall structure of the rites – was relatively uniform across Europe. Usually the body was taken from the home to the burial church in some sort of procession. At the church, the Office of the Dead consisted of a vigil service in the evening, followed the next day by the full requiem Mass. The body was then either interred in the church itself or taken, again in procession, to the cemetery for burial.

Funeral arrangements seem to have become more elaborate from the thirteenth century onwards. Accounts of increasingly grandiose occasions begin to survive from this date: the funeral of Sir John Hawkwood, the renowned English mercenary captain who led the Florentines to many victories during the 1390s, was one of the most dramatic examples. Fourteen caparisoned war horses were provided by the Florentine commune, the Guelph party and his own men, each with appropriate emblems. Hawkwood's body and the bier on which it rested were decorated with gold brocade and vermilion velvet. He held his sword on his chest and his baton in his hand. A massive number of mourners attended, all hooded in mourning clothes provided by the commune. The very fact that the events are recorded in such elaborate detail by contemporary chroniclers indicates that these arrangements were not typical, but they do show the level of spectacle that could be achieved in the funeral ritual of an important local figure.

Processions varied from a short journey to the local parish church with a few family members, to lengthy progresses that became both family and communal occasions. Giuliano de' Medici's funeral procession, which took place in Florence in 1516, was so long that the priests at the front had arrived at the church of San Lorenzo before the body had even begun to move from the starting point at the Badia de Fiesole. The long and indirect route passed places of significance to the family and was designed to mimic that of the triumphal procession of Pope Leo X, Giuliano's brother, three months earlier (see plate 49).

Although contrary to local regulation in Florence and Venice, corpses were frequently transported on biers exposed to full view. In these cases, the way the body was dressed was very important. Giuliano de' Medici's catafalque was surmounted by gold brocade curtains bordered with black velvet, while his corpse was dressed in gold brocade with full armour, and a cap that echoed his brother's papal tiara, with the heraldic lion of Florence. In contrast, some people rejected lavish dress in favour of the monastic habit. Simona di Tommaso Giovanni made this powerful statement by wearing the habit of an Augustinian nun at her funeral in Florence in 1434.

If the body was in a coffin, it could be covered in procession by a brightly coloured pall cloth. Only wealthy families owned their own palls. More typically they were borrowed from the parish or from a confraternity favoured by the deceased (see plate 26, page 34). Membership of a confraternity could also demonstrate the social power of the wealthy. In 1521, the Company of the Visitation of Our Lady in Florence provided a pall for Lisabetta Landini's funeral, as well as 40 priests, torches and 120 candles for the requiem Mass.

In French and English royal funerals it became normal to use a wooden effigy of the corpse. This lay on top of the coffin holding the actual body. Several survive in the collections at Westminster Abbey (see plate 50), some including death masks, cast from moulds taken directly from the face of the deceased. They were originally used for practical reasons, when the physical state of a body was not conducive to public display, and an elaborate court ceremonial built

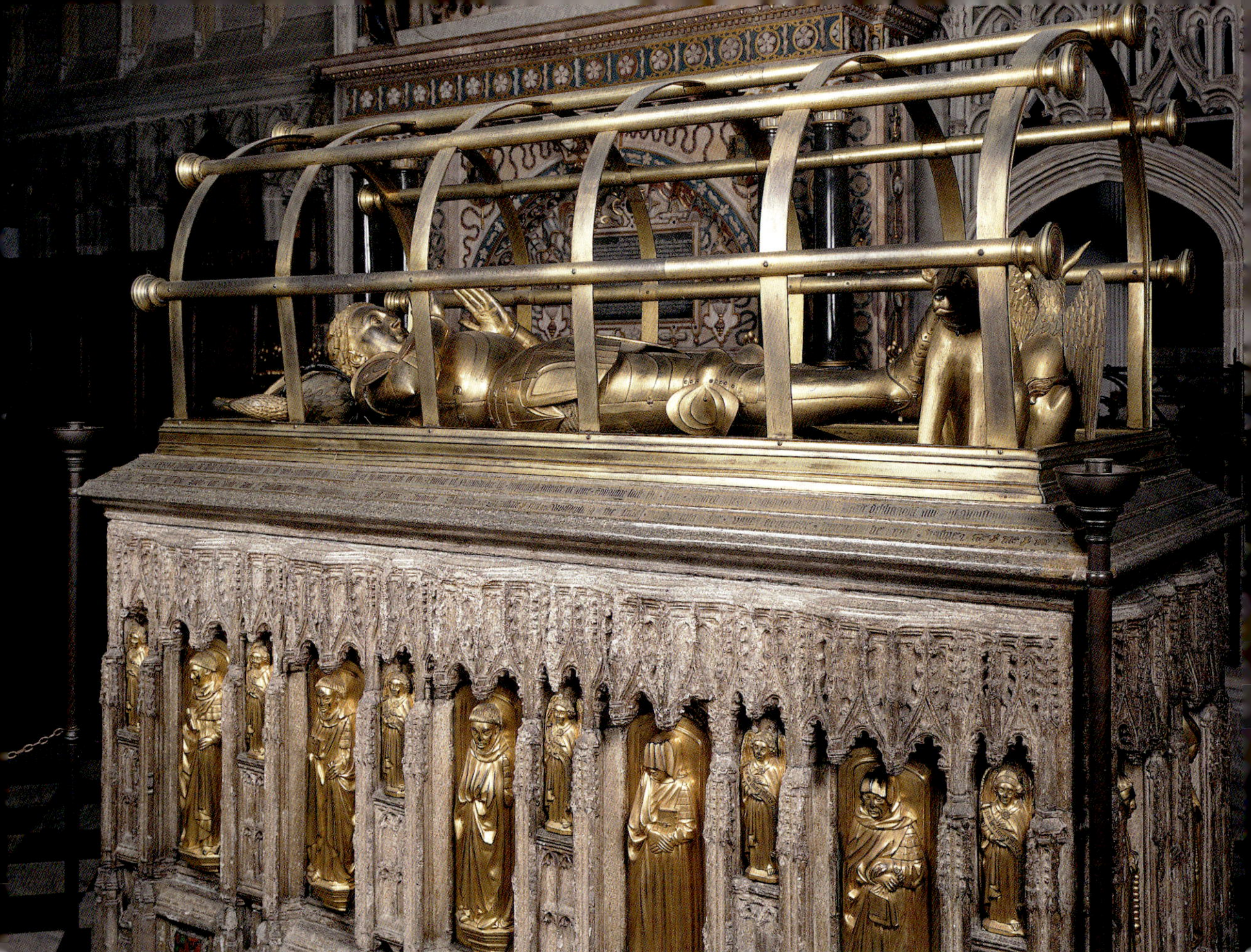



up around these effigies. Their realism created a fiction that the dead monarch was still alive, symbolizing the effective transfer of power between rulers without an interruption in sovereignty.

On arrival in church, the body was usually placed in a hearse (a wooden or metal frame) (see plate 51), which was covered in a pall and surrounded with candles. Mourners would group around it in black mourning garb (see plate 52). The text '*Placebo Domino in regione vivorum*' ('I will please our Lord in the land of the living'), based on the first part of the monastic service, Vespers, was recited and a vigil kept. The following day, the '*Dirige Domine Deus meus in conspectu tuo viam meam*' ('Direct, O Lord God, my way in thy sight'), the first part of Matins with

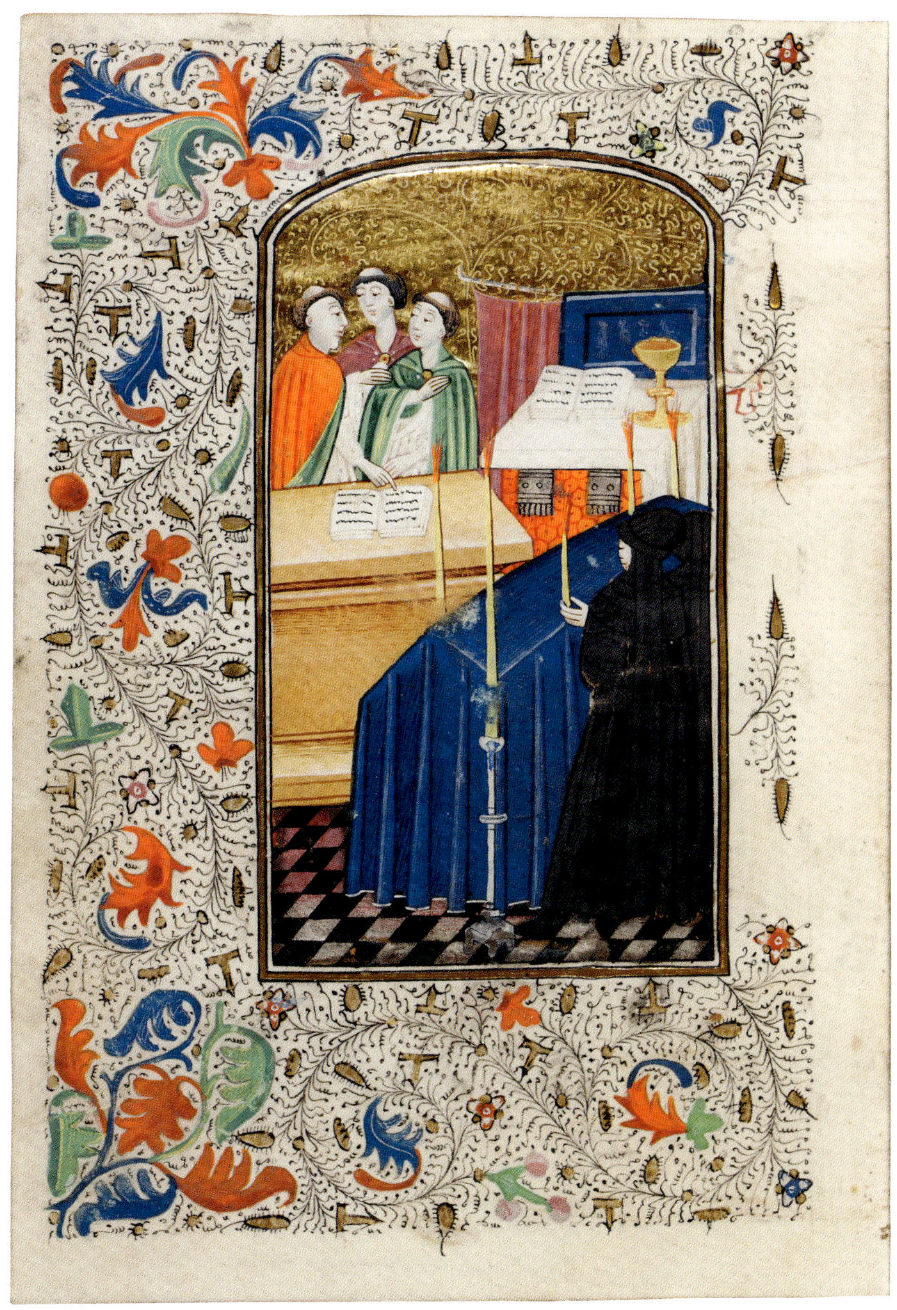

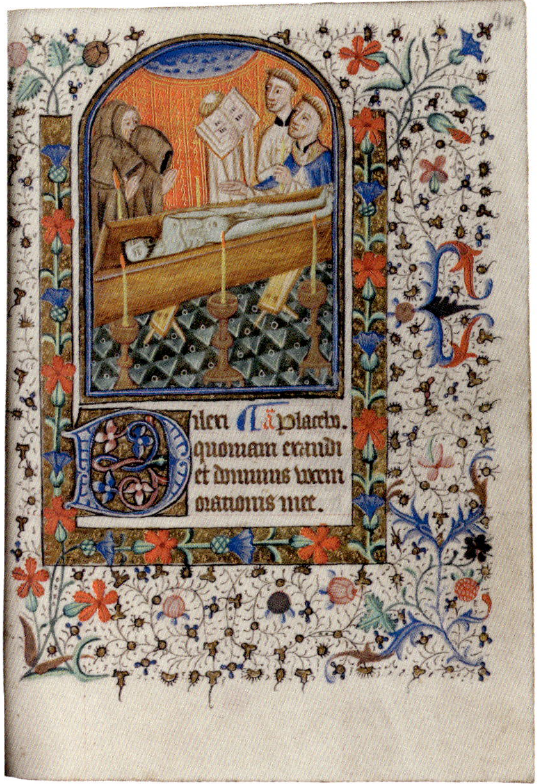

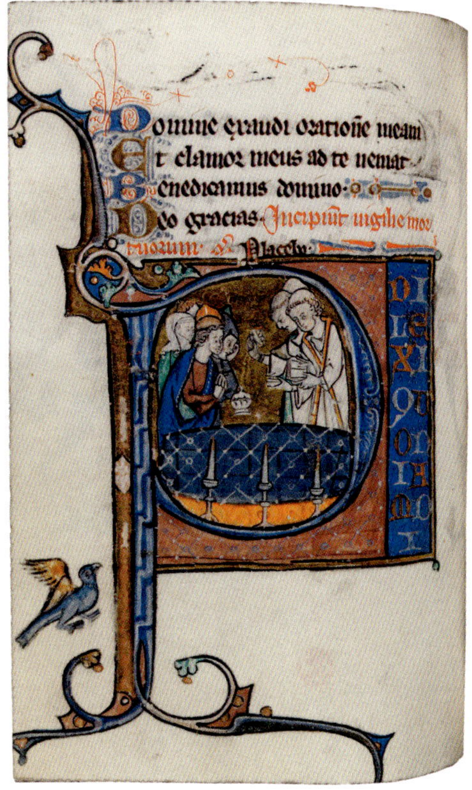



Lauds, was read directly before the requiem Mass. The requiem was intended to incorporate as many people as possible in a communal ceremony, including women, who were sometimes excluded from the procession. Candles, draperies and painted catafalques (funeral biers) promoted the status of the deceased, and were therefore often borrowed from the confraternities. Richer families could add sung Masses or organ music, or could increase the numbers and rank of clergy. Lorenzo de' Medici's funeral requiem in 1440 involved the Bishop of Valvi assisted by nine cardinals. Such augmentations of the basic rite would be expected to provide spiritual benefits for the deceased, as well as demonstrating the wealth and status they had enjoyed in life.

An enduring feature of funeral rites was the striking visual presence of the poor. In England and elsewhere, distribution of alms and clothes at funerals was

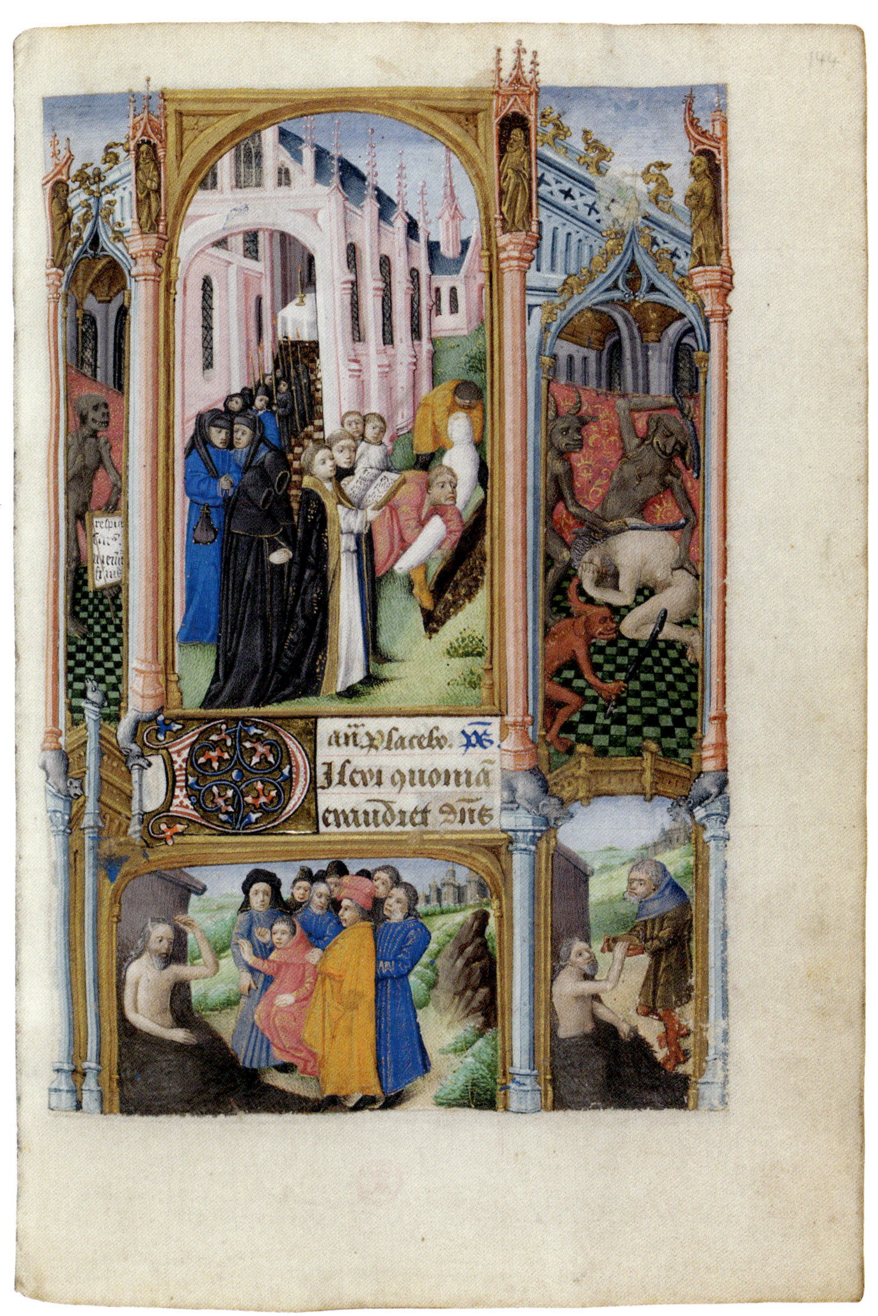
an̄ Placebo. ꝓ.
Dexi quoniā
exaudiet dn̄s

56
Burial scene from a book of hours;
illuminated manuscript, Paris or
Rouen (France), c.1500
(V&A: MSL/1902/1661, f.85)

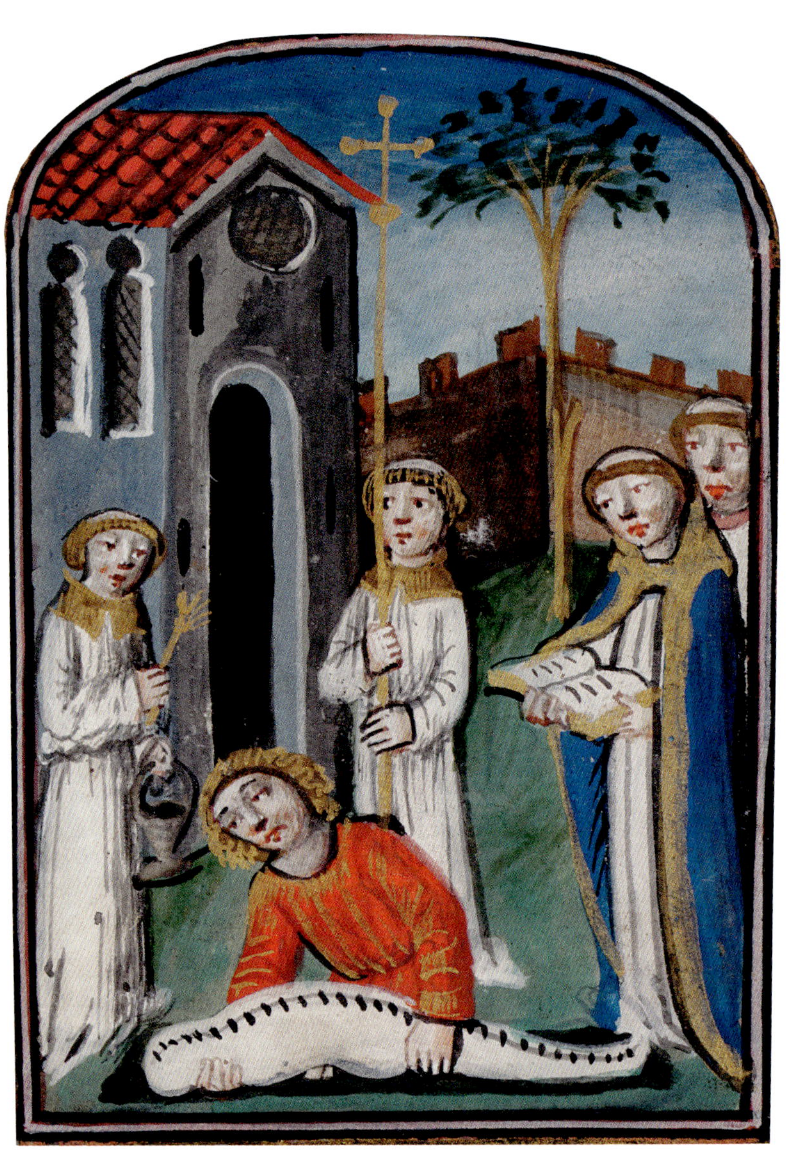

customary, and money was bequeathed by the dead person to the poor to attend their funeral to recite prayers. Often they stood around the coffin holding candles, wearing specific mourning garb if the deceased was wealthy – groups of such mourners are depicted in miniatures in books of hours (see plates 52 and 55). This demonstration of the charity of the dead person was particularly timely – the period after death was, after all, when the immediate fate of their soul was being decided in the Particular Judgement.

After the requiem, incense would be wafted over the body, and it would be sprinkled with holy water – a scene often depicted in books of hours (see plates 54 and 56). It would then be taken to the burial place; if this was in a separate cemetery, it could involve a further procession (see plate 55).

## BURIAL

I bequeath . . . my simple body to be buried at Humberston, in the chapel where both Margery and Anne my wives, and my natural cousin . . . and my son . . . lie buried, in such manner as my executors shall think appropriate for the rank to which it has pleased God to call me in this world, and to have there a fitting tomb for me and my wives

Will of Thomas Kebell of Humberstone, Leicestershire, 1500

The place of burial was thought to affect the fate of the soul after death, as well as reinforcing family and individual status. Before the thirteenth century, burial in cemeteries outside church buildings was the norm for all except senior churchmen, but from this period lay people began to press for burial inside the church – in England and France this followed royal precedent. Burial in the chancel (the holiest part of the church) was most prestigious, closely followed by burial before an altar or near images of the Virgin or favoured saints. The latter were believed to offer extra protection for the soul of the deceased. In larger churches there was a very specific order of precedence. At Canterbury Cathedral, the Black Prince (d.1376) originally requested a burial place near the cult image of Our Lady of the Undercroft, in the crypt. He was actually buried in an even more prestigious location next to the shrine of St Thomas à Becket, right in the heart of the cathedral.

There was strong competition for burial in the most important churches. During the fourteenth century, various regulations governed burial in the cathedral in Florence. Vieri de' Medici was allowed to display his arms and insignia on his tomb, but this could only be a pavement slab and could not be placed 'on the wall or in a prominent space'. Burial in Franciscan and Dominican churches

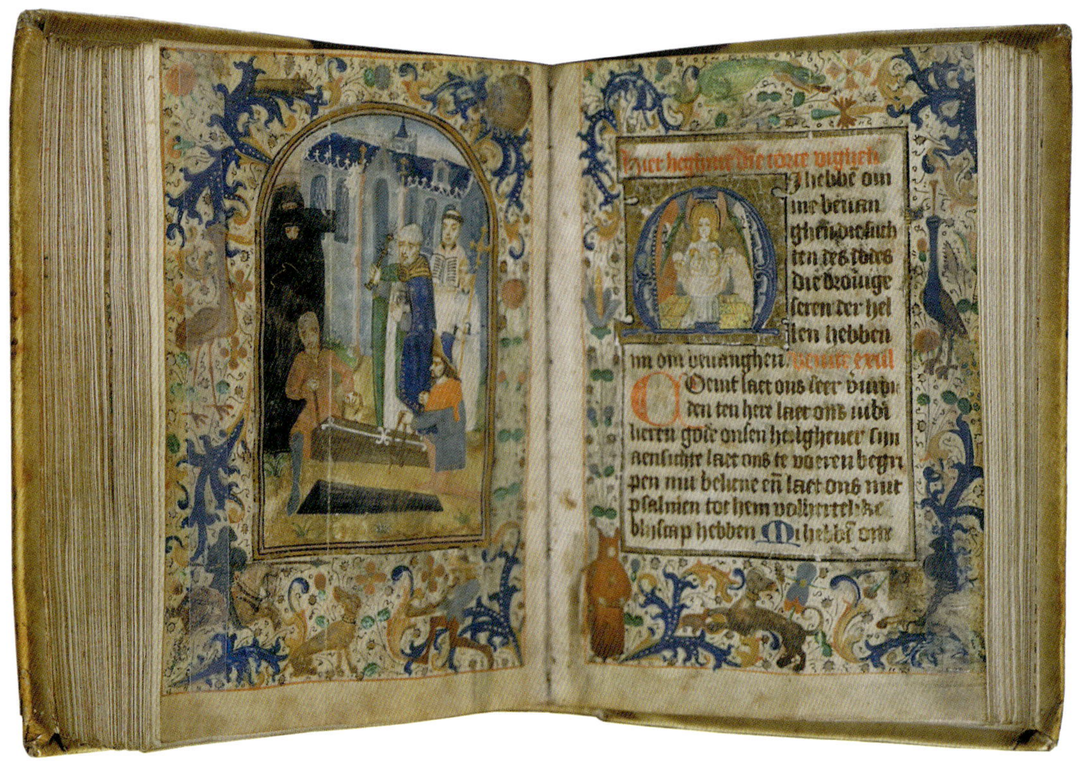

57
Burial scene from a book of
hours; illuminated manuscript,
Netherlands, c.1475
(V&A: MSL/1854-7-4, pp.288–9)

became popular, following the rise of those orders. The rector of the small parish of San Donato dei Vecchietti in Florence complained in 1427 that his parishioners preferred to be buried at Santa Maria Novella, the Dominican church, diverting valuable revenue from his own church.

A similar hierarchy governed the best places to be buried outside church. The area immediately surrounding the chancel was particularly favoured, as was burial in the cloister of monastic houses. At the lowest end of the social scale, poorer people usually ended up in temporary graves in a cemetery, marked with a simple stone or wooden cross – these graves would be emptied after a certain number of years, and the bones stored in the parish charnel house. Florentine criminals without private tombs were buried in the common cemetery outside the city gates, and the corpses of those who were not Florentines were sometimes offered for dissection by anatomy students.

It is not surprising that individuals of means preferred burial in places with strong family associations. In Douai, Flanders, wills stressed burial alongside one's spouse, while in central Italy the preference was for family crypts, tombs or chapels. Sometimes great trouble was taken to bring bodies back over long distances. The inscription on the tomb of Richard Beauchamp, Earl of Warwick, in St Mary's church, Warwick (see plate 51, page 58), describes how, after his death at Rouen in 1439:

> The which body with great deliberation and full worshipful conduct by sea and by land was brought to Warwick the third day of October the year above said and was laid with full solemn obsequies in a fair chest made of stone in this church.

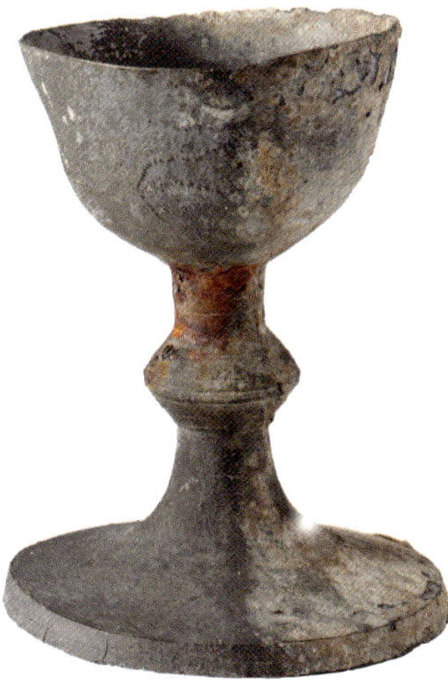

58
Chalice thought to have been found in 1832 in the tomb of the Abbot of St Vanne (d.1452) at Verdun; pewter, France, 1300–50
(V&A: 72–1904)

Once the corpse had reached the burial site, psalms and antiphons (responses) were sung or recited as the grave was opened. It would be sprinkled with holy water, blessed and censed, and the body laid in it (see plate 56). Usually the body was simply in a shroud by this stage, though coffins were sometimes used, generally by wealthier people (see plate 57). In spite of laws passed between 1293 and 1473 specifying burial in a simple linen shirt, archaeological evidence shows that Italian corpses were usually buried in the clothes they had been dressed in for the funeral (with any associated insignia, or symbols of personal office). This projected the social identity of the dead into the afterlife. French and English kings were also buried with their insignia until the late fifteenth century. When the tomb of Edward I (d.1307) in Westminster Abbey was opened in 1774, his body was found wrapped in a waxed linen cloth, wearing red and gold royal robes with a crimson mantle and a gilt crown, and holding an enamelled sceptre. Abbots and bishops were also customarily buried with symbols of their office, and chalices, crosiers and mitres – often replicas made in base metal – have been excavated from tombs in England, France and elsewhere (see plate 58).

To give the soul the best possible chance of progressing safely to Heaven, it was customary for memorial Masses, or obsequies, to be said for the deceased. The minimum would be a Mass one week, one month and on the first anniversary after the death. The deceased might be represented symbolically on these occasions by a hearse, draped with a pall. The arrangements became increasingly elaborate. The trental (Masses for each of the 30 days after death) was particularly popular, but many wealthier believers specified more than this. A friar from the Carmine church in Florence, Fra Nicola, said 100 Masses for the soul of one of his relations during the plague of 1348/9. In 1400, Jehan de Roquignies requested vigils and Masses on the day of his death in all the churches and friaries of Douai; and by 1500, Thomas Kebell, an English lawyer, was requesting 1,000 Masses to be said immediately on his death, with each priest receiving fourpence. He also specified daily Masses for seven years afterwards. This development probably reflected a combination of factors, including an increasing belief in the efficacy of Masses in alleviating the torments of Purgatory, as well as the need to promote family and community status.

Wills showed real concern about whether the required number of Masses would actually be celebrated. Thomas à Kempis warned: 'Do not put your trust in friends and relatives . . . for men will forget you more quickly than you think' (*The Imitation of Christ*, 1:23). On All Souls' Day, obsequies would be celebrated for all dead people, ensuring some level of blanket coverage. Membership of a religious confraternity also provided some insurance. The Guild of the Holy Cross at Stratford-on-Avon, Warwickshire, established by 1269, employed chaplains to say Mass for the souls of members both alive and dead in their guild chapel and at altars supported by the guild in the local parish church.

Monasteries had been a major generator of prayers and Masses for the dead, but as the doctrine of Purgatory became accepted from the thirteenth century, lay people began to take more responsibility for their own spiritual welfare. A family, confraternity or individuals could pay a priest to say Masses for their souls after death: such endowments were called chantries. This followed royal example: Edward I made elaborate arrangements for Eleanor of Castile's

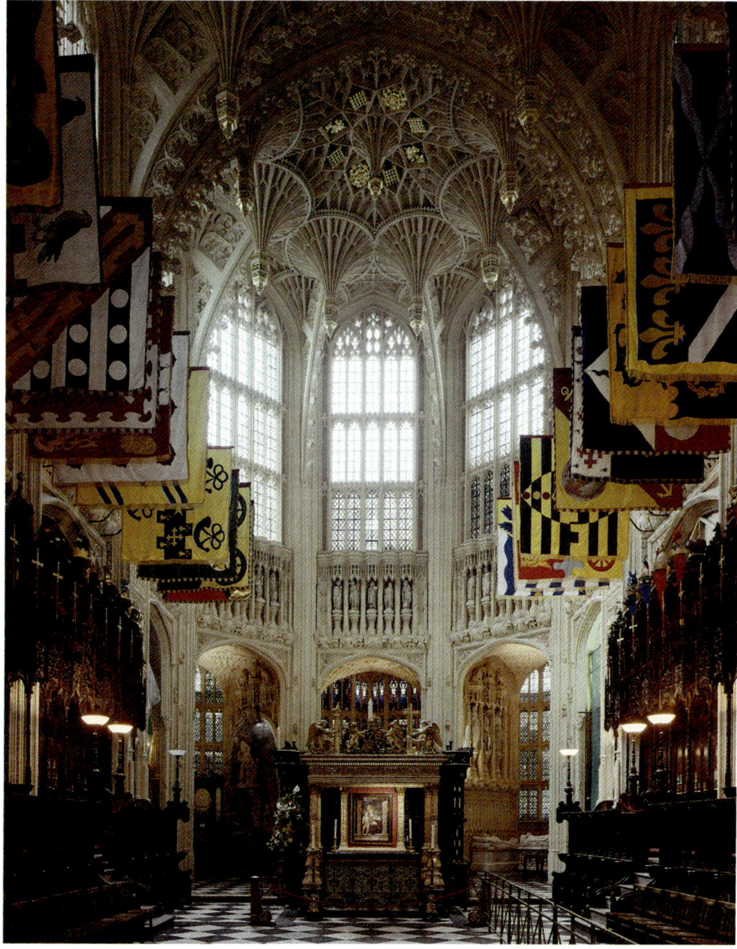

soul after her death in 1290, including endowments for Masses in perpetuity, with priests installed in four locations. Increasingly such Masses were celebrated in chantry chapels, specific spaces within larger churches that ranged from relatively simple wooden enclosures fencing off an area inside the existing church to grandiose additions to the exterior of churches, with ornate window tracery and carefully selected stained glass and sculpture (for example plate 59). By endowing these spaces, pious individuals could do their utmost to ensure ultimate salvation for their soul in an uncertain world.

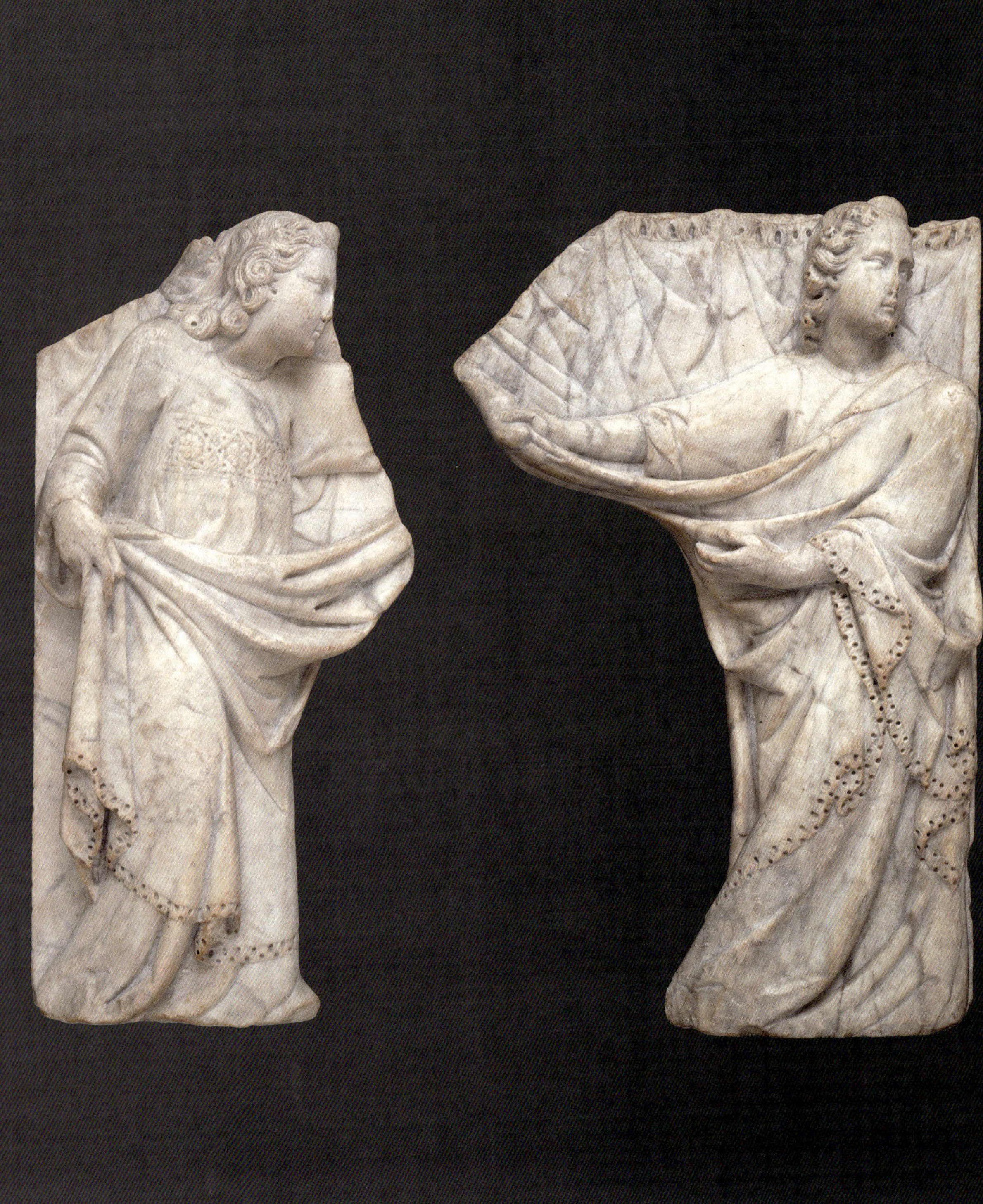

# CHAPTER 4

# Tombs and memorials



It had long been important in the Christian tradition to mark the place of burial. With the gradual movement of graves inside churches from the thirteenth century, a tradition of impressive tombs developed. Monuments could also be placed elsewhere in memory of the dead person.

Both tombs and monuments performed multiple roles. They were intended to stimulate prayers for the soul of the dead person, as well as act as *memento mori*, encouraging the onlooker to contemplate his or her own mortality. Additionally they promoted remembrance of the deceased in life, and of their social position as noble, knight, bishop, and so on, enhancing their status and that of their family. The balance between these functions changed over time and according to geographical location. Although the celebration of social position and worldly achievement has been associated with the advent of the Renaissance, people had been memorialized according to their role in life for many years beforehand. Knights from England to Italy were traditionally shown in full armour (see plate 61 and plate 62). Initially such celebration was often intended to contribute towards obtaining salvation after death. The thirteenth-

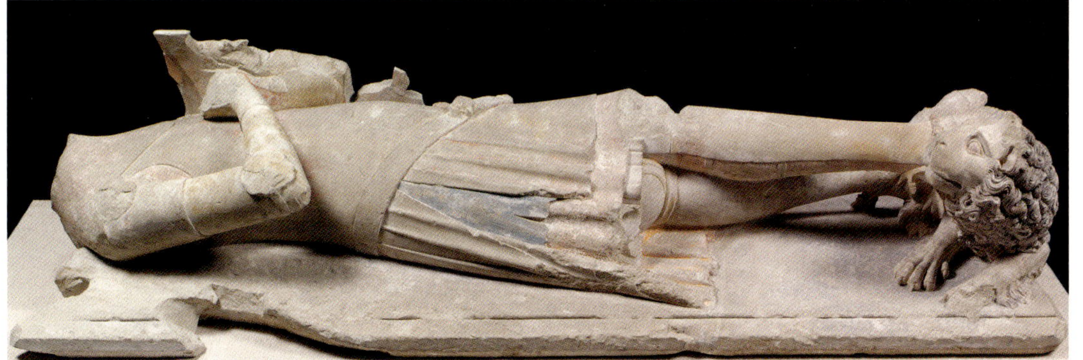

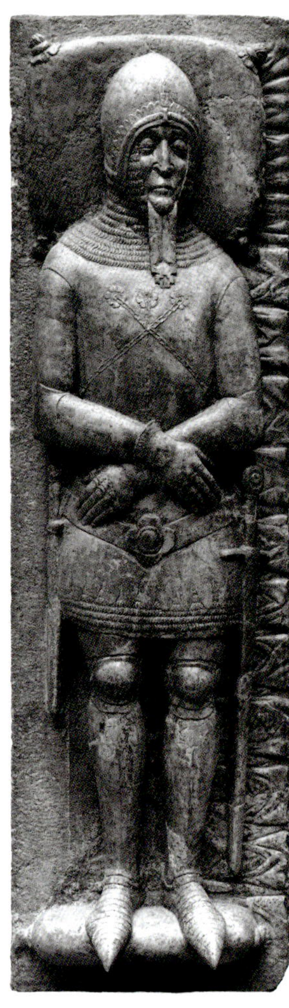

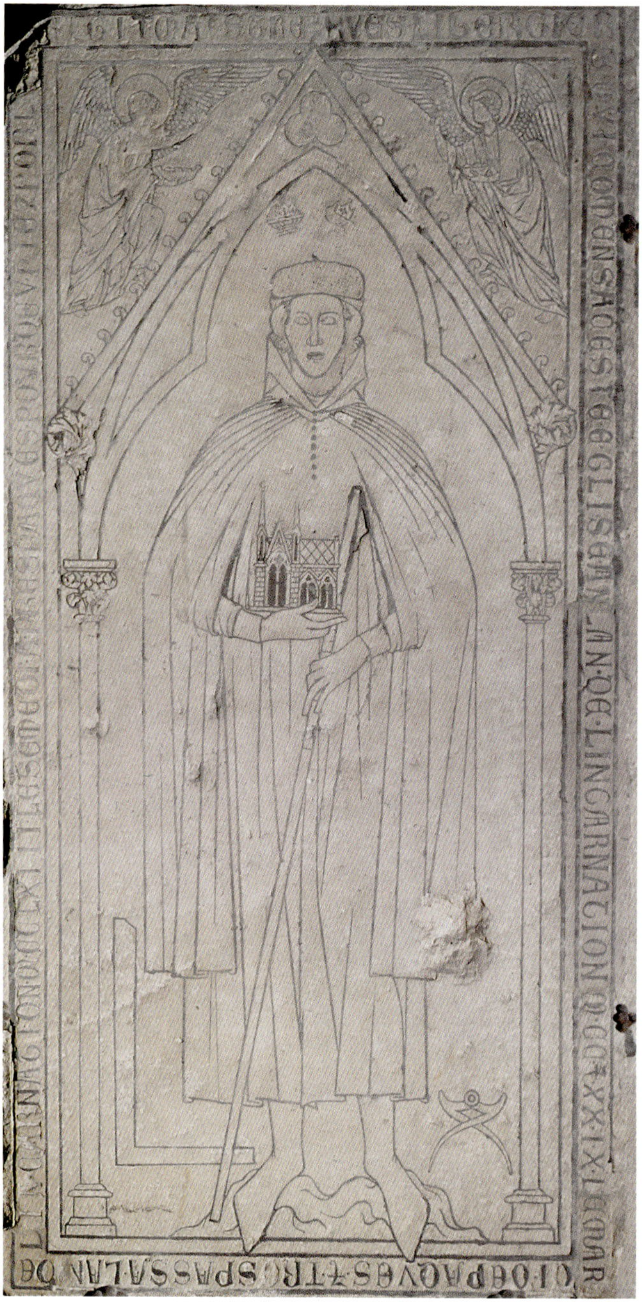

62 ABOVE
Effigy of an anonymous knight; Istrian
stone, Veneto (Italy), c.1370–75
(V&A: A.24–1910)

63 RIGHT
Incised slab showing Hughes Libergier
(d.1263); stone inlaid with black niello
paste, Reims (France), 1260s
(Reims Cathedral, France)

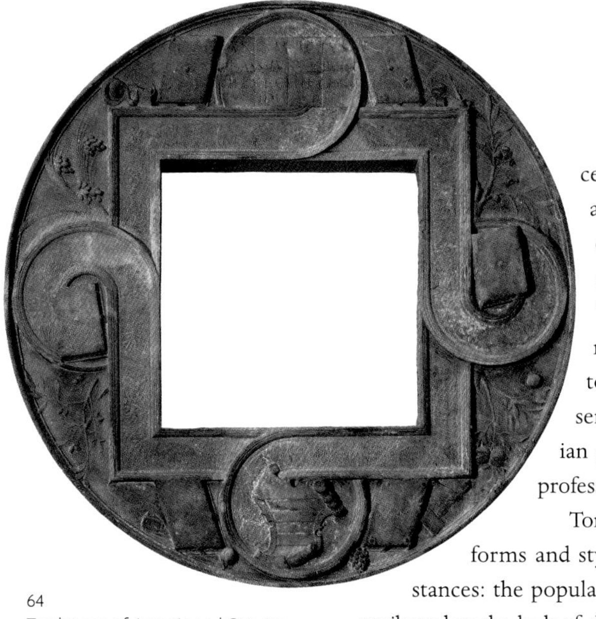

64
Tombstone of Antonio and Caterina
Maggi da Bassano, probably by
Vincenzo and Gian Matteo Grandi;
Istrian stone, Padua (Italy), 1520
(V&A: 71–1882)



Translation of part of a Latin
inscription on a brass to John
and Agnes Browne of Stamford,
Lincolnshire, c.1476

century incised slab showing Hughes Libergier, the architect of the abbey of Saint-Nicaise at Reims (plate 63), shows him with the tools of his trade and holding a model of the abbey, designed for the glory of God. The use of emblems to denote one's station in life remained popular into the sixteenth century and came to have an almost purely secular function: the books, serpent, parchment rolls and inkwell on an unusual Italian gravestone all refer to Antonio Maggi da Bassano's profession as a lawyer (plate 64).

Tombs and monuments survive in an incredible variety of forms and styles. Often these are the result of practical circumstances: the popularity of wall tombs in Venice, for example, has been attributed to the lack of deep earth for the crypts that were popular elsewhere in Italy. But certain features and types appeared all over Europe, designed to maximize the chance of salvation for the deceased or to proclaim their status.

## TOMB SLABS AND BRASSES

Bodies buried inside churches tended to be in the ground, or shut away in vaults. The earliest internal markers were therefore slabs, flush with the ground, which covered these graves – they literally marked out the space of the grave, though not all were of the usual rectangular shape (see plate 64). Generally they were orientated on a west–east axis, towards the high altar at the east end of the church. Slabs seem to have appeared in the eleventh century and then enjoyed a long, unbroken tradition right through to the 1500s, sometimes appearing on walls as well as the floor. From the late 1100s onwards, images of the full-length figure began to appear on these slabs, usually incised into the surface of the stone, and sometimes marked out by the use of a black paste or cement known as 'niello' (plate 63). These were widely used in France and Italy.

Incised slabs were also popular in England (plate 65), where from the late 1200s makers experimented with inlaying parts of the figure with metal plates.

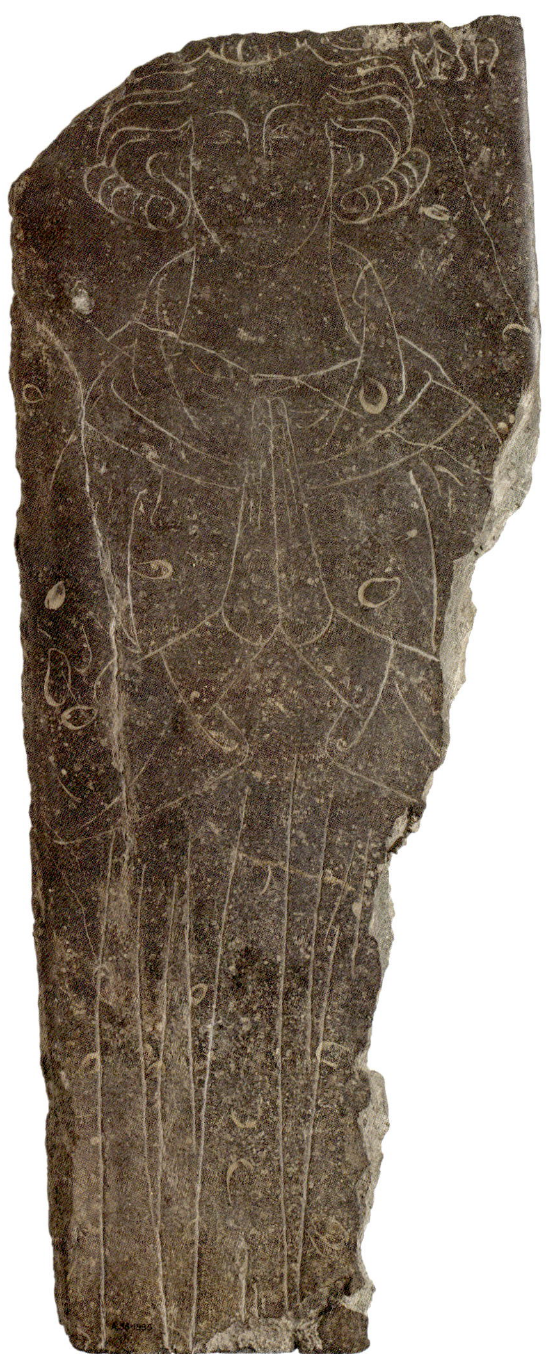

65
Incised slab showing a male figure;
Purbeck marble, London (England),
*c.*1320
(V&A: A.53–1935)

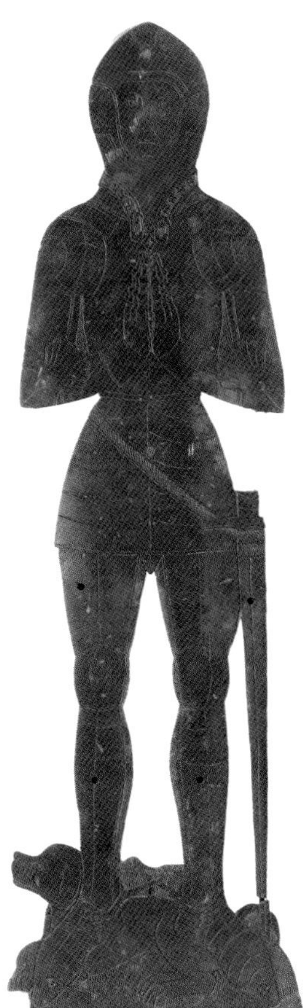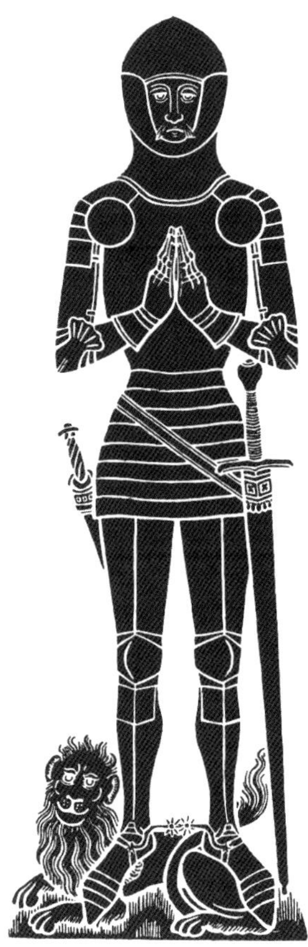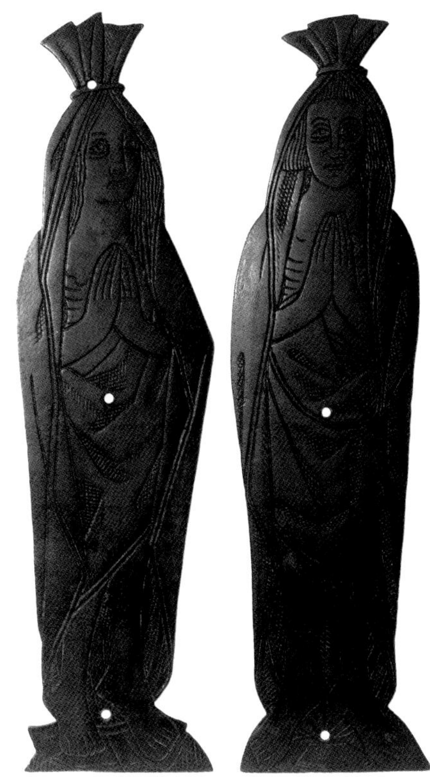



Ultimately this practice led to figures laid out entirely in brass, known as monumental brasses. Incised slabs and monumental brasses were probably produced in the same workshops for at least the first half of the fourteenth century. Initially these brasses were commissioned mainly by clerical and lay elites, but by the end of the 1300s they had become a relatively cost-effective means of commemoration that was attractive to a wider range of patrons. One reason was the increase in standardized representations, which permitted an element of mass production (see plate 66). Often those represented were depicted as knights in armour or in rich clothes, but a fashion also developed for representing the dead in their shrouds. Robert Alee chose to have himself and his two wives shown in this way (plate 67) – their open eyes indicate that they are depicted at the

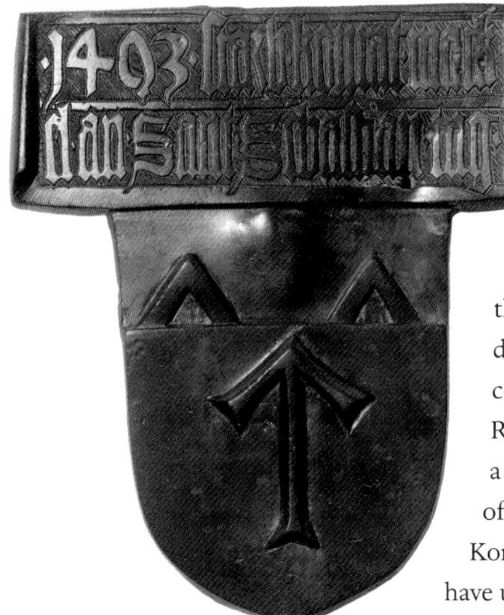

68
Grave tablet of Konrat Mackel;
bronze, Germany, 1493
(V&A: M.27–1953)

69 OPPOSITE
Rubbing of monumuental brass
to Robert Braunche and his
wives; brass, Netherlands, 1364
(St Margaret's church, Kings Lynn, Norfolk)

moment of resurrection. Figurative brasses are often (even usually) accompanied by an inscription identifying the deceased and requesting prayers for their soul (see plate 44). Increasingly, on tombs generally as well as brasses, these inscriptions were in the vernacular language of the country concerned (see plates 68 and 80), reflecting an increase in literacy across Europe during the 1400s.

Brasses were not only popular in England. In the Netherlands and the Rhineland incised brass plates of increasing sophistication were produced, usually with full background decoration incorporated. These continental brasses were popular exports: the spectacular brass of 1364 to Robert Braunche and his two wives at St Margaret's church, King's Lynn, is a typical example (plate 69). Metal was also used in tablets fitted to the lids of tombs or slabs, or mounted on the wall to identify graves. The tablet of Konrat Mackel, a German merchant, replaces the heraldry that a noble would have used as identification with his merchant mark and an inscription declaring that he died on St Sebastian's day, which was intended to stimulate prayers for his soul (plate 68).

FREE-STANDING AND WALL TOMBS

Initially only saints had free-standing, three-dimensional tombs. But gradually, during the twelfth and thirteenth centuries, the papacy and then royal figures adapted these forms for their own use. It is likely that slabs were first raised from floor level for practical reasons – many surviving floor slabs are very worn – as well as to increase the prominence of the tombs of eminent figures. Initially they were raised up on short columns, sometimes shaped as animals, and then on the tomb chests that became ubiquitous, particularly in northern Europe. A huge range of forms developed, both free-standing and mounted against walls. Wall tombs, which were particularly popular in Italy and France, appeared from the twelfth century onwards. Often their designs were dictated by the practicalities of display in a church crowded with other tombs, though certain consistencies emerged that indicate concerns common throughout Christendom.

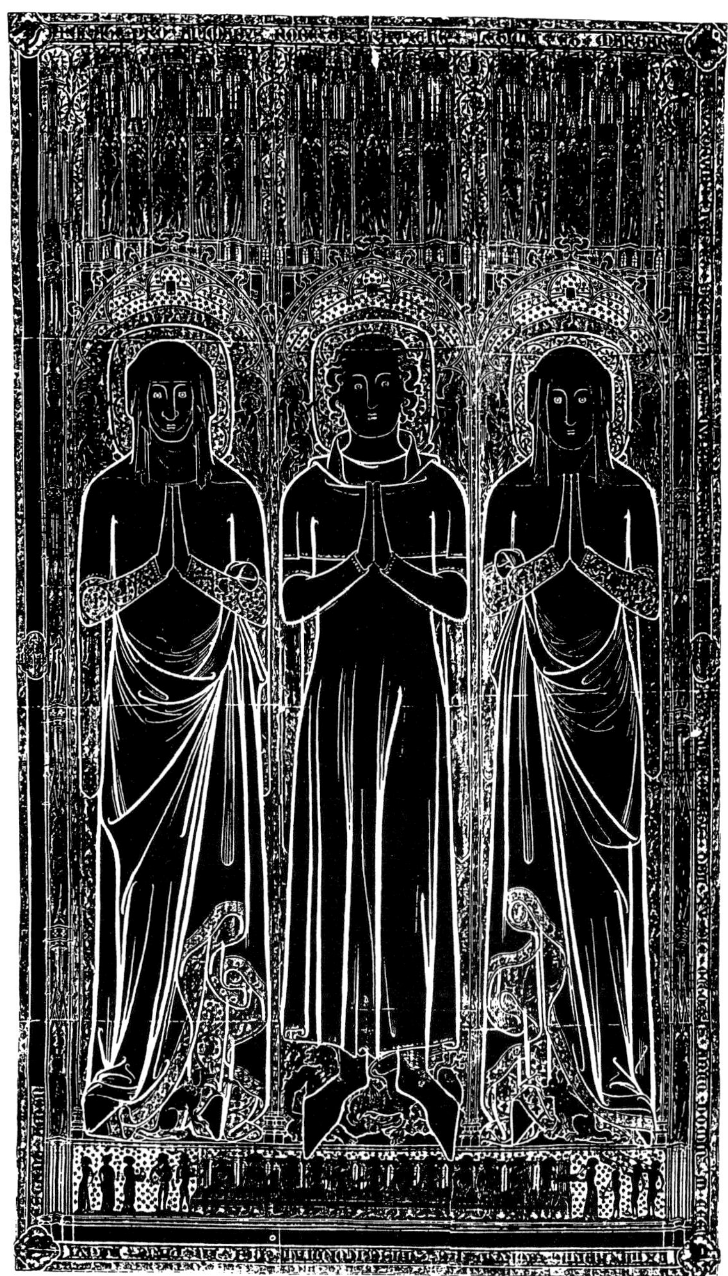

70

Tomb to a member of the Percy family;
stone, after 1340

(Beverley Minster, East Yorkshire)

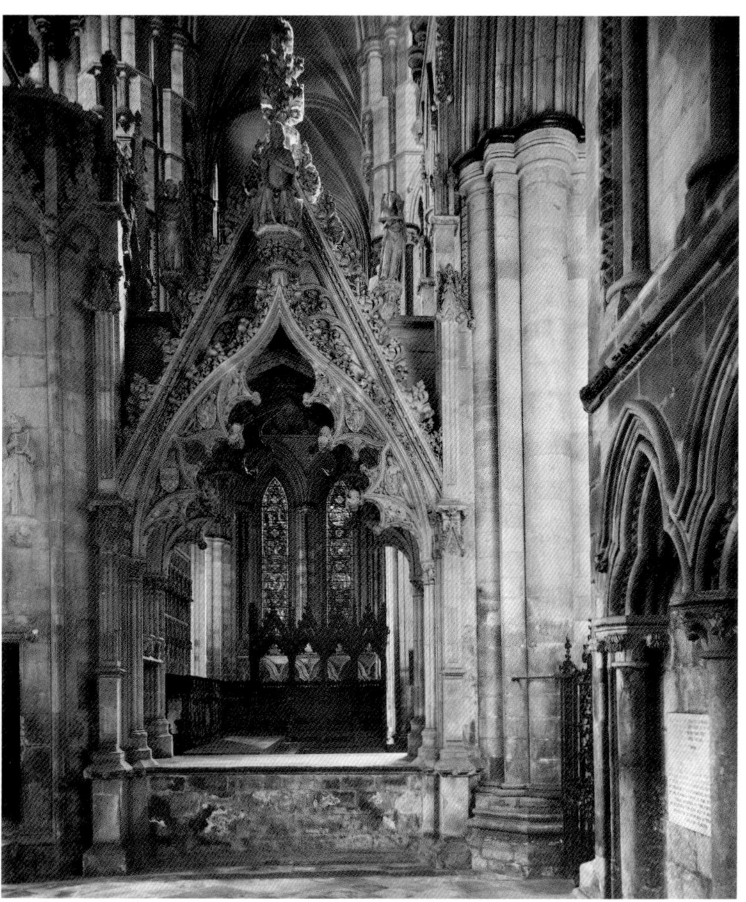

Canopies were used to set apart certain spaces as special and divinely favoured. Ciborium canopies were placed over high altars, and canopies of state over the thrones of kings and high nobles. Similar canopies swiftly became an important feature of the grandest tombs. One of the most extravagantly decorated ones covered the Percy tomb in Beverley Minster, East Yorkshire (plate 70).

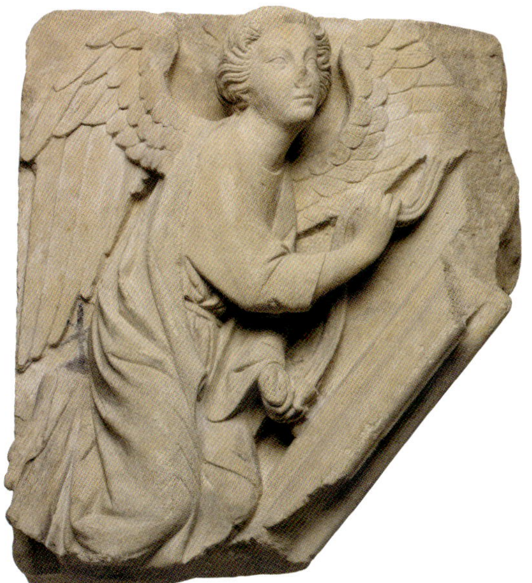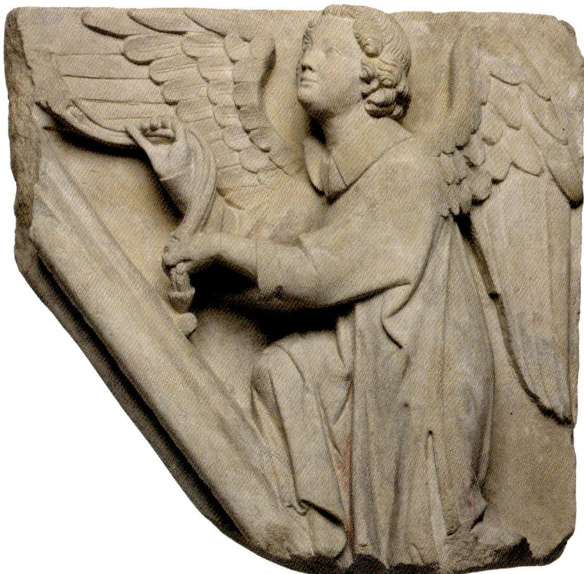

71
Angels from a tomb canopy;
Dolomite limestone, probably
Lincoln (England), *c*.1270–80

(on long-term loan to the V&A from the Rector,
Parochial Church Council and Church Wardens of
the Parish of Sawley, Derbyshire)

Canopy decoration could further identify the space of the tomb as sacred: angels swinging censers (plate 71), like those from a tomb at Sawley, Derbyshire, reflected funeral ceremonial, while characteristic Italian angels drawing back curtains to reveal the effigy added a theatrical touch to wall tombs (see plate 60, page 68).

WEEPERS

In the late 1200s, small-scale mourners or 'weepers' began to be placed along the sides of tomb chests – they seem first to have appeared in French royal tombs, but the fashion spread across Europe (apart from Italy), particularly from the late fourteenth century. These figures could be angels (plate 72), clerics or members

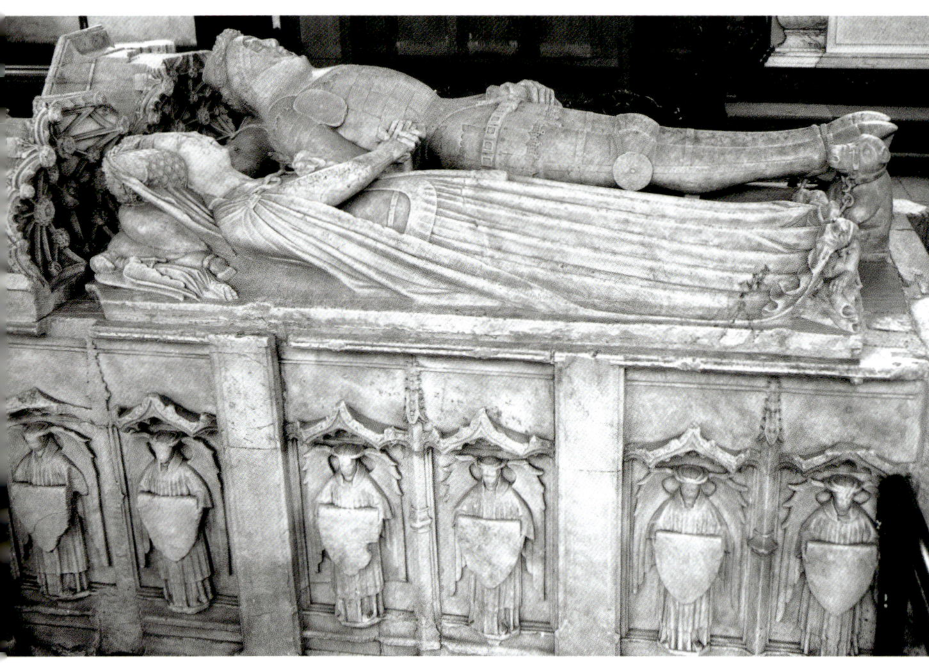

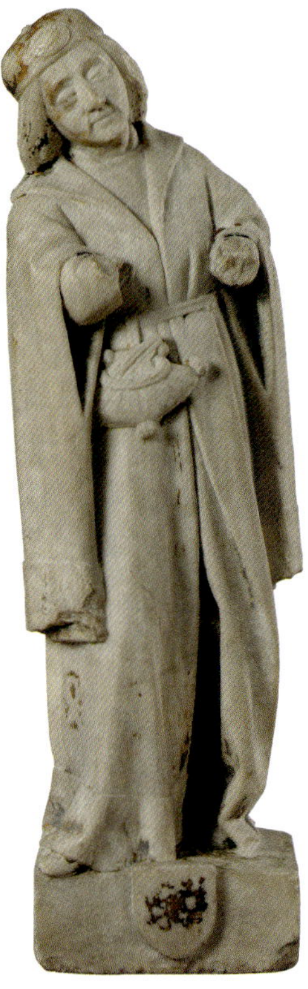

72 ABOVE
Effigies of Ralph Greene and Katherine
Mallory, by Thomas Prentys and
Robert Sutton; alabaster, Chellaston,
Derbyshire (England), 1419–20
(St Peter's church, Lowick, Northamptonshire)

73 ABOVE RIGHT
Weeper; alabaster, Dijon or northern
France, c.1440–60
(V&A: 4084–1857)

74 OPPOSITE
Weepers from the tomb of Philip the
Bold, workshops of Claus Sluter and
Claus de Werwe; alabaster, Dijon
(France), c.1400–10
(Chartreuse de Champmol, Dijon)

of the family or retinue of the deceased. The last-named are usually identified
by shields, which would have been painted with the appropriate coat of arms
(see plate 73). By the later fifteenth century they were appearing in bronze as well
as stone, as on the tomb of Richard Beauchamp at Warwick (plate 51, page 58).

Weepers functioned on several levels: family members bolstered the status
of the deceased with their dynastic support, while clerical and angelic mourners reflected funeral liturgy, and that of memorial Masses taking place around
the tomb. The famous weepers from the tomb of Philip the Bold, who was
buried in a Carthusian habit at Dijon (plate 74), include Carthusian monks whose
cloaked figures directly reflect the mourning garb that was such a strong visual
feature of the medieval funeral (see plate 55, page 61).

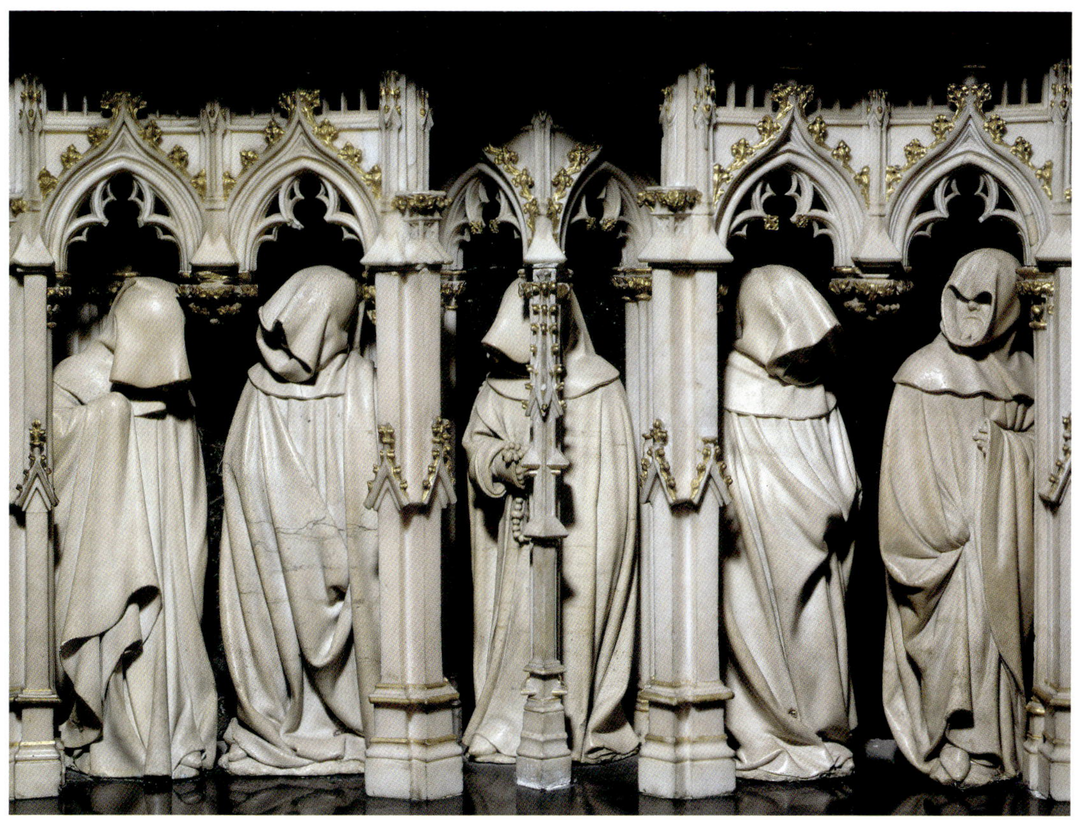





Including an image of the deceased on a tomb identified the person being com-memorated, stimulating remembrance and, of course, prayers for their soul. Effigies were not an essential feature of tomb design before the late thirteenth century, particularly on Italian tombs and those for lay patrons. Figures carved in outline on flat slabs gradually developed into effigies sculpted in the round, a change intimately connected with the development of the three-dimensional tomb from the two-dimensional tomb slab. These lifelike figures quickly became prevalent from the late 1200s onwards.

A variety of materials was used for effigies: examples are found in stone, marble, alabaster, metal and wood. The choice of material depended partly on what was available locally, with Purbeck marble and alabaster from Staffordshire and Derbyshire being favoured in England, and Istrian stone a popular choice in northern Italy. It was also partly a question of fashion, with the use of alabaster spreading rapidly in England after it was employed for several royal effigies in the early 1300s, such as the tomb of Edward II at Gloucester. Sometimes the choice had a particular significance. Gilded bronze had strong royal associations in England, being used for several kings' effigies from Henry III (d.1272) onwards. As a result, leading nobles became keen to use this expensive combination of materials to illustrate their links to the Crown: the effigy of Richard Beauchamp (see plate 51, page 58), friend of Henry V and guardian to the young Henry VI, is also in gilded bronze. Cost would have been another factor. Because effigies were often covered in a layer of gesso (plaster) and then painted, the use of wood became a viable alternative to other, more expensive materials. The gesso layer could itself be used to provide an extra level of detail: the stone de Lucy effigy has chainmail patterns stamped into its gesso (see plate 61, page 69). The effigy or tomb could be further embellished using enamels or coloured stones: the Black Prince's gilded latten tomb at Canterbury Cathedral has both types of ornamentation.

It is often hard to be certain whether effigies are meant to be portraits or generic representations. Even an effigy as convincing as that of Richard Beauchamp, made approximately 10 years after his death in 1439, may not have been a true likeness of the man himself. The use of death masks as models for some Italian effigies as early as the fourteenth century indicates that a true likeness was seen as important there earlier than it was in northern Europe. The creators of the effigy of Bishop Salomone Castellano (d.1322) at Treviso Cathedral used casts not only of his face, but also of his hands. Interest in portrait effigies came to northern Europe more slowly. We know from comparison with other portraits of Richard II (d.1400) that his tomb effigy at Westminster Abbey is a portrait. Indeed, the contract specified that the effigy should 'reproduce the body of our said master the King', and the point was reiterated in the accounts for payment. But at the same date, and in the same country, the popularity of increasingly standardized monumental brasses indicates that portrait effigies were not the norm (see plate 66, page 73).

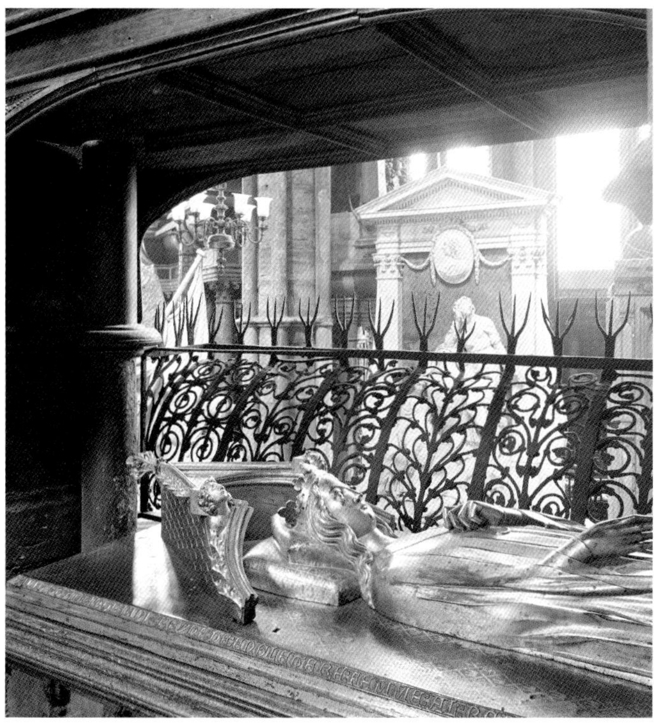

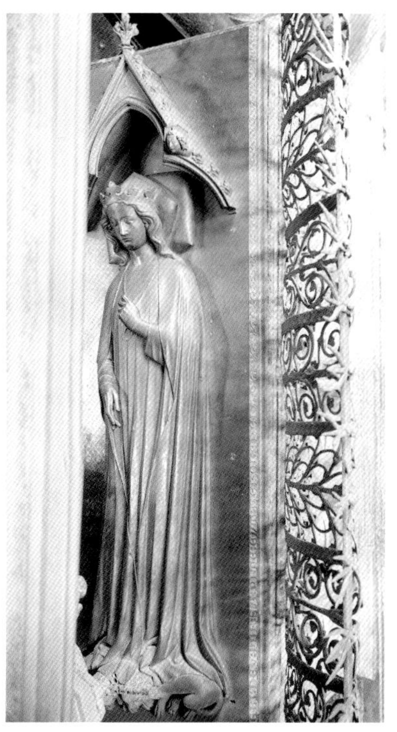

75

Effigy of Queen Eleanor, by William
Torel; gilded bronze, *c.*1290

(Westminster Abbey, London)

The detail (left) shows the tomb as
it is in the abbey. A view from above
(right) shows how the queen's drapery
is shown as if she were standing upright.

It is also not always clear whether an effigy is meant to represent the person as dead or alive. In many effigies, the horizontal position of the figure on the tomb (emphasized by features such as a pillow beneath the head) is at odds with a design that firmly depicts a vertical figure, with drapery falling towards the feet and an architectural canopy over the head (plate 75). Generally in northern Europe, at least until the fifteenth century, the norm was to represent the figure with its eyes open, and hence presumably alive. The inclusion of features related to funerary ritual, such as censing angels and pillows, has led to the suggestion of links with wax or wooden funerary effigies, where the eyes were sometimes open. In Italy, where the use of effigies during funerals was less usual,

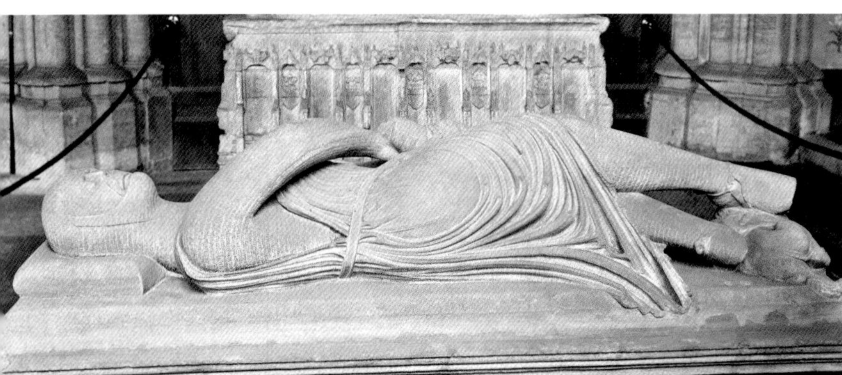
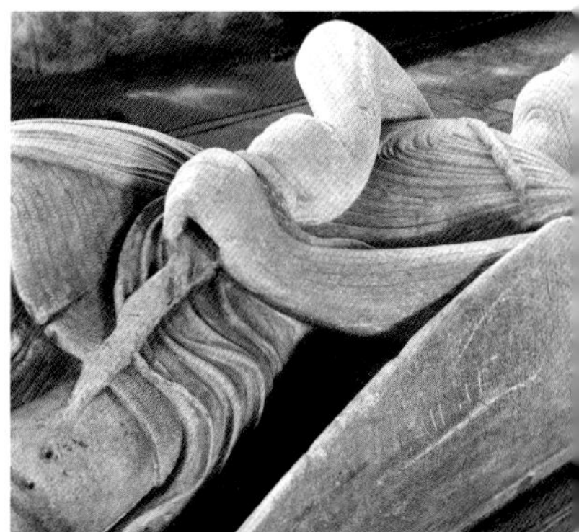

76
Effigy of an anonymous knight; stone,
England, late 13th century
(Dorchester Abbey, Oxfordshire)

the norm seems to have been to represent the person as dead, or at least asleep (see plate 62, page 70). The Italian knight shown in that image is represented as an old man, with his face sunken in death, lying on a bier cloth. He also has his hands crossed, in what became a standard pose for Italian effigies.

Poses could vary considerably. A series of English knights was produced during the 1200s with crossed legs, twisting and struggling to draw their swords (plate 76) – the motif of crossed legs continued in use for knightly effigies into the 1300s (see plate 61, page 69). Husband and wife were sometimes seen holding hands, symbolizing their marriage, as at Lowick (plate 72) – the same motif appeared in monumental brasses. Gradually the standard pose for the recumbent effigy became one of prayer, intended to stimulate the prayers of others.

Although recumbent effigies remained the norm in northern Europe well into the sixteenth century, gradually figures of the deceased began to be depicted in other ways: kneeling, reclining and even enthroned in majesty. The equestrian figure, echoing the Roman type for celebrating military leaders or rulers, reappeared in Italy. It was particularly popular in Verona (see plate 77), following the series of elaborate external monuments to members of the della Scala family erected outside the church of Santa Maria Antica. Sometimes these new poses were simply a response to the practical problem of visibility, as tombs became more elaborate and effigies were elevated, making recumbent figures less visible

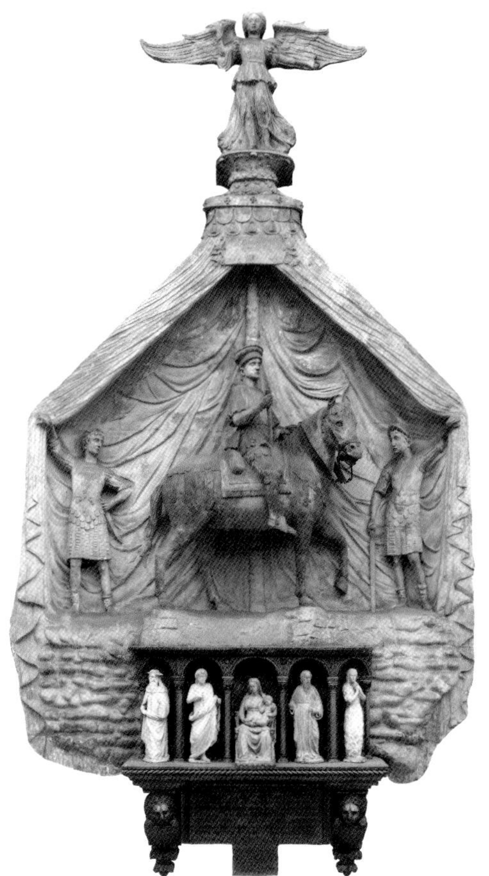

from below (plate 84). The initial Italian solution of tipping up the recumbent effigy (for example plate 62, page 70) did not become widespread.

Effigies would be suitably dressed: ecclesiastics were clad in clerical dress, knights in armour and noble women in elaborate, fashionable outfits. This custom may have related to that of burying suitable identifiers with the body (see page 65), reflecting a belief that one's position in a hierarchical society was somehow echoed in the afterlife. Sometimes specific features were included to indicate a biographical detail: the anonymous knight in a monumental English brass (plate 66, page 73) wears the collar of SS that was worn by supporters of the Lancastrian cause in fifteenth-century England. Often dress was used to indicate the piety of the dead person: Don Garcia de Osorio wears the mantle of the

78
Effigies of Don Garcia de
Osorio and Doña Maria de
Perea; alabaster, Toledo
(Spain), 1499–1505
(V&A: A.48 and 49–1910)

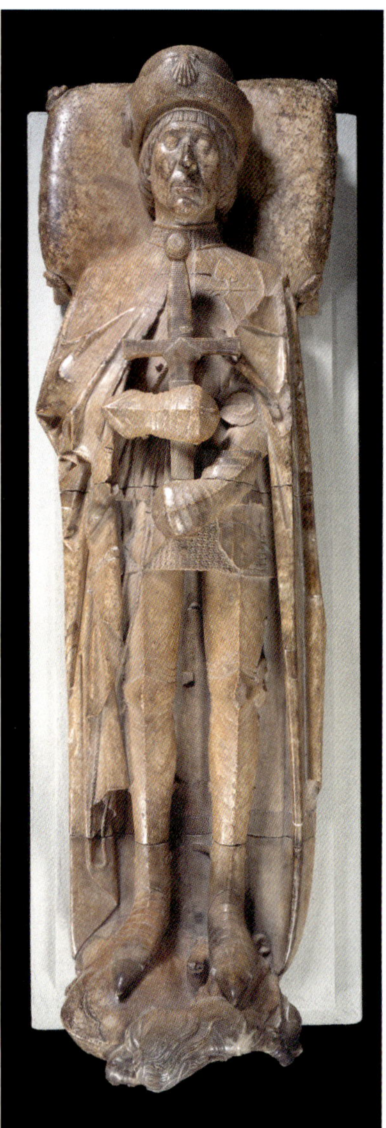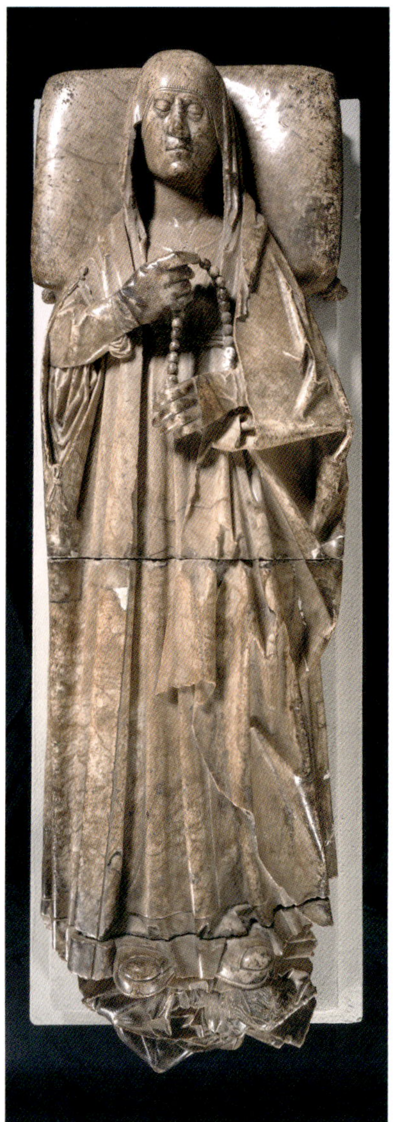

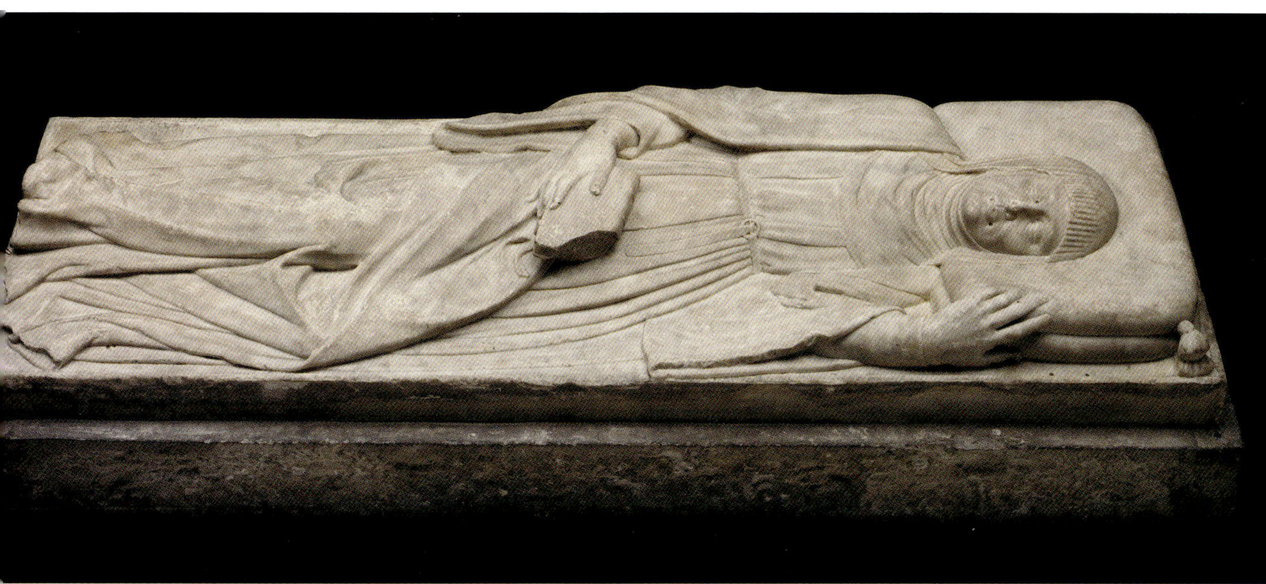

79
Effigy of a woman; marble, Naples
(Italy), *c.* 1500–10
(V&A: 7388–1861)

Order of Santiago, a chivalric order dedicated to the Christian cause, with its cockle-shell badge in his hat, while his wife, who clutches her rosary, is deliberately shown in humble dress, with plain wooden shoes to emphasize her modest piety (plate 78). Sometimes effigies wore the habits of particular religious orders: a Neapolitan woman, for example, is dressed in the habit of a Tertiary (plate 79), a lay member of a religious order. Burial in such clothes was believed to confer spiritual benefit (see page 57).

This contrast between promoting an image of stately dignity and one of humble piety reached its ultimate expression in the *transi* tombs that appeared in France, England and the Holy Roman Empire for two centuries from the late 1300s. These usually juxtapose two images of the dead person: one in the full panoply of their worldly status, with another of their dead body, seen as a corpse or even a skeleton. The grandest tombs in both countries favour a double-decker arrangement, with the naked corpse represented below the fully dressed figure

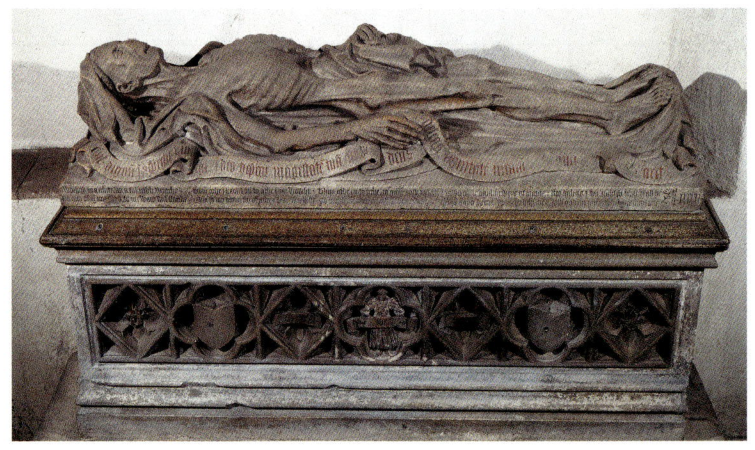

80
Tomb of John Baret, limestone tomb chest with traces of paint and Purbeck marble effigy, probably Bury St Edmunds (England), 1450s
(St Mary's church, Bury St Edmunds, Suffolk)

(plate 30, page 38). Some tombs feature only the cadaver effigy (plate 80), although even then it could be juxtaposed with an image of the deceased in life. John Baret, depicted as an emaciated corpse on top of his tomb chest, is seen in life on the front, as a small-scale figure wearing a fur-trimmed gown and a collar of SS. Such images reminded onlookers of their own mortality, stimulating prayers for the soul of the person depicted. This was particularly significant when they were created during the lifetime of the person being commemorated. Archbishop Chichele (d.1443) would have been able to contemplate his own cadaver (his effigy was complete by 1426) and ponder on an uncertain future after death. One of several Latin inscriptions laments: 'Now I am cast down: and turned into food for worms.' Another specifically requests prayers from onlookers:

> Whosoever you are who will pass by [here], I ask for remembrance from you
> You who will be like me, you who will afterwards die
> Horrible in everything – dust, worms, vile flesh.

The phenomenon is not found in Italy, where representations of corpses or skeletons tend to represent Death himself, rather than a specific named individual.

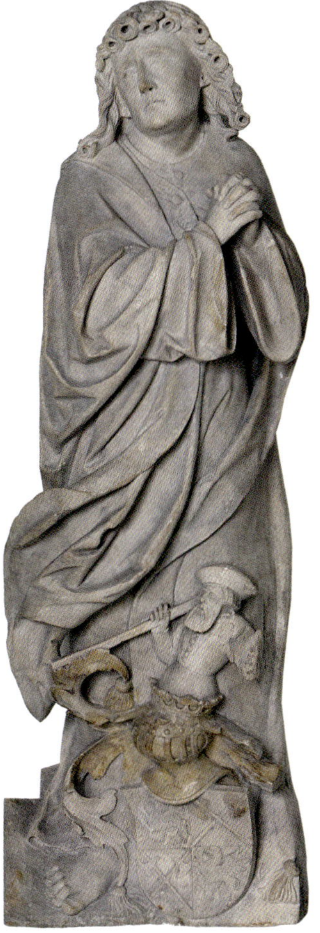

81
St John the Evangelist, from a
Crucifixion epitaph group by Hans
Daucher; limestone with traces of
gilding and paint, Germany, c.1523
(V&A: 49–1864)

## OTHER GRAVE-MARKERS

The fear of burial in a mass grave, with the associated lack of funeral rites and memorial Masses, was felt all over Europe after the Black Death first appeared in 1348 and stimulated an increasing interest in marking one's grave out from others. This did not need to be by means of an elaborate tomb or effigy. In 1348 Nullus, son of Pepi, commissioned a Maestà (Virgin in Majesty) for 10 lire to hang above his grave in the village church in Castellone, Italy. Wills in Douai, Flanders, also show testators increasingly commissioning images (usually sculptural reliefs) of themselves and their spouses to identify their graves.

Funeral accoutrements, particularly banners or heraldic shields, were customarily placed around or over the tomb. The achievements (helmet, surcoat, shield, gauntlet and sword scabbard) of the Black Prince are still displayed near his tomb in Canterbury Cathedral. Heraldry was used by families to stake a claim to space within the church – coats of arms could appear on walls, pillars, altars and furnishings. This space was then jealously guarded. The will of wool merchant Agostino di Francesco di Ser Giovanni specified that the friars of Santo Spirito, Florence, were not permitted to place any flag or any shield next to his chapel, in an attempt to preserve as many sightlines into his chapel and tomb as possible.

## MEMORIALS

Commemorative monuments honour an individual in a specific place associated with them, separate from their burial site. The monument to Spinetta Malaspina (plate 77), for example, was built by his heirs to commemorate his role as founder of the church in which it was placed: S. Giovanni in Sacco, Verona.

Epitaphs – wall-mounted slabs of stone with an image of the deceased, usually at prayer either before a devotional image or in a narrative scene – first appeared in the fourteenth century. They were particularly popular in sixteenth-century northern Europe, appearing up to the eve of the Reformation. This figure of St John the Evangelist (plate 81) by Hans Daucher comes from the

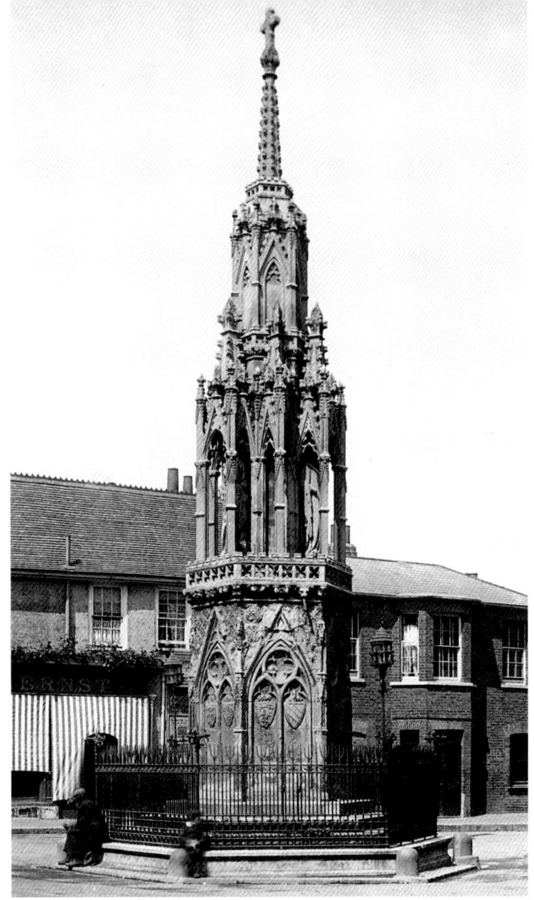

82
Eleanor Cross, designed by Roger
of Crundale and sculpted by
Nicholas Dymenge; limestone,
England, 1291–4/5
(Waltham Cross, Hertfordshire)

Crucifixion group on an epitaph commemorating Gregorius Lamparter. The
epitaph was originally intended for a church in Nuremberg, but was actually
installed in a church near Augsburg because family members feared attacks
from reformers.

Some memorials were exceptional in their grandeur and ambition.
Eleanor of Castile, wife of Edward I, died near Lincoln in 1290. While her
entrails were left for burial at Lincoln Cathedral, her embalmed body was
brought back to London for burial at Westminster Abbey in 12 stages. At each
resting place the king commissioned an elaborate stone cross to be erected in
her memory and to elicit prayers for her soul. Three of the crosses survive (see
plate 82); they were probably inspired partly by the stone *montjoie* memorials
used to mark the funeral route of the French king, Louis IX, in 1270. Eleanor's
heart was buried at the Dominican church at Blackfriars, London. The lavish

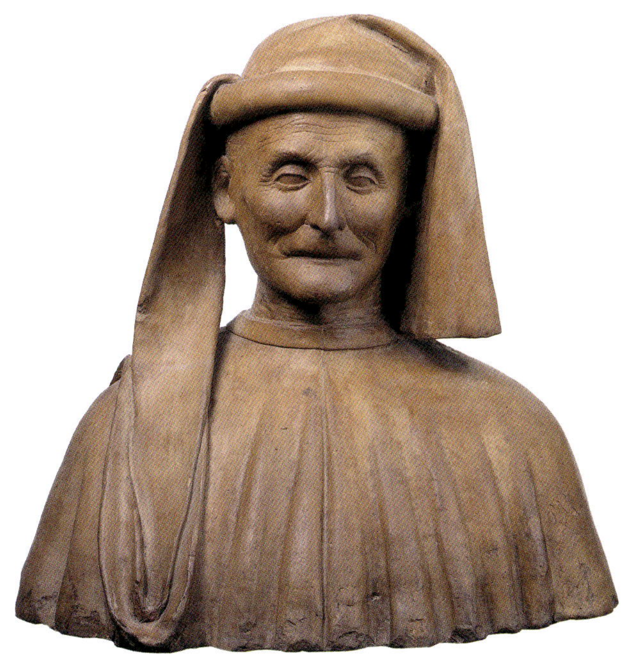

83
Bust of a member of the Capponi
family; terracotta, Florence (Italy),
1450–1500
(V&A: 7588–1861)

scale of this memorial exercise, unprecedented in England, indicated the loss of
a wife 'whom living we dearly cherished, and whom dead we cannot cease to
love' (letter from Edward I to the abbot of Cluny, 1291), as well as being an
explicit statement of royal status.

In Italy, commemorating family members took forms distinct from the
rest of Europe. Two main types of commemorative image became popular in
Florence during the fifteenth century. Busts of dead members of the family
based on classical prototypes were used to provide a visual history of the family
and to promote family tradition – they were placed in the home above chimney-
pieces, doors, and so on. The Capponi family commissioned a series of busts to
decorate the library of their family house (see plate 83). The face of this example has been modelled from a death mask, indicating the importance attached
to obtaining a true likeness for succeeding generations. Such images were

84
Tomb for a member of the Moro
family; Istrian stone, porphyry and
marble, Venice (Italy), 1500–50
(V&A: 455–1882)

entirely secular in their motivation but, in a parallel development, images of family members in relatively low-cost materials like wax, terracotta and papier mâché were placed in churches. These were intended to elicit prayers from the living and give thanks to the saints, as well as to perpetuate a living likeness for posterity. Although relatively few survive, the scale of the practice is confirmed by written records: in 1447, the church of Santissima Annunciata, Florence, had to add two large shelves to the walls of the tribune to accommodate the growing number of figures.

The sixteenth century brought changes to tombs and monuments in northern and southern Europe. In Italy, interest in various classical forms continued to intensify. A tomb produced for a member of the Moro family in the early sixteenth century (plate 84) combines the traditional recumbent effigy with a sarcophagus featuring a porphyry roundel and a classical inscription. Although iconography reflected ever-increasing interest in commemoration over more purely religious motivations, Counter-Reformation Italy contained many tombs that combined the secular (from personal commemoration to Neoplatonic ideas) with orthodox Christian subject matter.

In northern Europe the traditional table and wall tombs, often featuring recumbent effigies, continued in production, but in areas where the Reformation took root the rationale behind them was transformed. The sole purpose of these structures became the commemoration of the life of the individual, rather than the stimulation of prayers for their soul.

# Conclusion

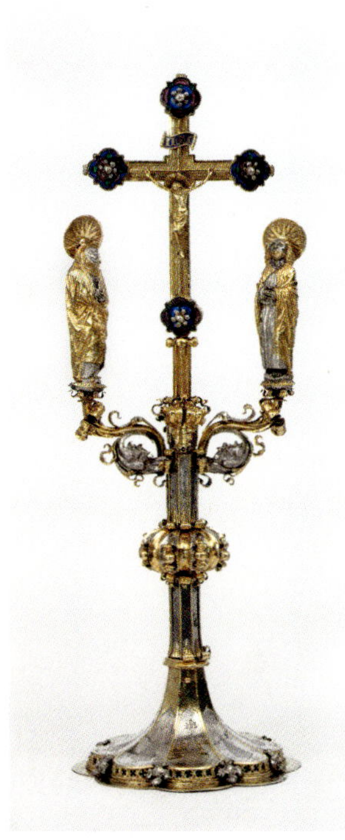

85
Reliquary cross; silver and gilded silver with translucent enamel and pearl, Basel (Switzerland), cross: 1350–1400, base: *c.*1477

(V&A: 7939–1862)

From the 1520s onwards, reformers in northern Europe challenged many of the core Christian beliefs that had shaped responses to death, and their effects on works of art.

Criticism of the indulgence system, one of the central themes of the Reformation, focused particularly on the selling of indulgences, which had become a more regular practice over time and underwrote many commissions of art and architecture, particularly during the fifteenth and early sixteenth centuries. The base of a reliquary cross from Basel (plate 85), for example, was paid for by the selling of indulgences.

Protestant reformers believed that faith alone could save the soul from the torments of Hell. Martin Luther declared passionately, 'Death, sin, and hell will flee with all their might if in the night we but keep our eyes on the glowing picture of Christ and his saints and abide in the faith, which does not see and does not want to see the false pictures.' The concept of Purgatory, and the resulting conviction that the actions and prayers of the living could help the souls of the dead, was particularly targeted as Catholic superstition. Without these beliefs there was no point to any of the apparatus that had supported efforts to limit the time spent by individual souls in Purgatory.

In contrast, in the parts of Europe that remained Catholic (in particular Spain and Italy), belief in Purgatory was reinforced in response to the advent of Protestantism. In these areas, artistic production was still motivated by traditional concerns, although commemoration of the individual continued to gain ground as a primary motivator in tombs and monuments.

During the early sixteenth century, beliefs surrounding death underwent a total transformation over large parts of Europe. Though the fear of death in an uncertain world was still a feature of daily life, the means of dealing with it had changed for ever.

# Further reading

Most of the titles listed in the General section below explore one or more of the specific issues that are examined in detail in the other sections.

GENERAL

Ariès, P., *The Hour of Our Death*, trans. H. Weaver, New York, 1981 – a broad sweep, exploring attitudes to death from classical times to the present day

Binski, P., *Medieval Death: Ritual and Representation*, London, 1996 – an in-depth exploration of beliefs surrounding the afterlife, representation and commemoration, as they developed throughout the Middle Ages

Boase, T.S.R., *Death in the Middle Ages: Mortality, judgement and remembrance,* London, 1972 – this 35-year-old study is still a useful and highly illustrated introduction to the subject

Daniell, C., *Death and Burial in Medieval England 1066–1550*, London, 1997 – an accessible examination of the English experience of death in the Middle Ages

Duffy, E., *The Stripping of the Altars: Traditional Religion in England c.1400–c.1580*, New Haven and London, 1992, Chapters 9 and 10 – looks specifically at popular belief in late medieval England, much of which held true for elsewhere on the Continent

Gordon, B. and Marshall, P. (eds), *The Place of the Dead: Death and remembrance in late medieval and early modern Europe*, Cambridge, 2000 – quite specific case studies, but a useful general introduction

Huizinga, J., *The Autumn of the Middle Ages*, Chicago, 1996 – this famous elegiac description of the end of the Middle Ages (first published in Dutch in 1919) portrays the medieval world as obsessed with death; its central premise has been much debated ever since

Jupp, P.C. and Gittings, C., *Death in England: An Illustrated History*, Manchester, 1999, Chapters 4 and 5 – a fascinating background to the English experience of death from the twelfth to the sixteenth centuries

Vovelle, M., *La Mort et l'Occident: de 1300 à nos jours*, Paris, 1983 – another wide-ranging exploration, and (with Ariès) one of the most influential studies of the subject

RELIGIOUS BELIEF

Delumeau, J., *History of Paradise: The Garden of Eden in Myth and Tradition*, Urbana and Chicago, 2000 – explores the different elements that made up the medieval conception of Heaven

Geary, P., *Living with the Dead in the Middle Ages*, Ithaca, 1998 – examines the relations between the living and the dead, which developed particularly with the advent of Purgatory

Jezler, P., *Himmel, Hölle, Fegefeuer: Das Jenseits im Mittelalter* [Heaven, Hell, Purgatory: The Afterlife in the Middle Ages], exhibition catalogue, Schweizerischen Landesmuseums etc., Zurich, 1994 – full of fascinating visual evidence for the various beliefs surrounding the afterlife, with particular emphasis on Germany

le Goff, J., *The Birth of Purgatory*, trans. A. Goldhammer, Chicago, 1984 – an influential exploration of the emergence of the doctrine of Purgatory, which was to prove so key to the effects of death on the arts

Swanson, R.N., *Indulgences in Late Medieval England: Passports to Paradise?*, Cambridge, 2007 – a useful study of indulgences and their effects on religious practice

Vauchez, A., *Sainthood in the Later Middle Ages*, trans. J. Birrell, Cambridge, 1997 – demonstrates how a belief in the intercessionary powers of these heavenly helpers affected religious culture of the period

IMAGERY OF DEATH

Olds, C.C., Williams, R.G. and Levin, W.R., *Images of Love and Death in Late Medieval and Renaissance Art*, exhibition catalogue, University of Michigan Museum of Art, 1976

Scaramella, P. et al., *Humana Fragilitas: The themes of death in Europe from the 13th century to the 18th century*, Clusone, Italy, 2002

Richardson, C., 'Art and Death', in *Viewing Renaissance Art*, ed. K. Woods, C. Richardson and A. Lymberopoulou, New Haven and London, 2007, pp.207–245 – explores attitudes towards death and commemoration in fourteenth and early fifteenth-century Europe through close examination of specific works of art


FUNERARY PRACTICE

Horrox, R., *The Black Death*, Manchester, 1994 – an enlightening collection of primary sources, which describe the horrors of the Black Death and its impact on the usual funeral ceremonies

Strocchia, S.T., *Death and Ritual in Renaissance Florence*, London, 1992 – a study of one city, which sheds light on practice throughout Italy


TOMBS AND MONUMENTS

*Grove Dictionary of Art*, Oxford, 1996 (also available online, with a PIN from your local library) – useful general articles about tombs, monuments and memorials

Panofsky, E., *Tomb Sculpture: Its changing aspects from ancient Egypt to Bernini*, London, 1992 – this far-reaching study traces a progressive change in tomb iconography from an earlier forward-looking focus on ensuring salvation to an increasing emphasis on looking back at the achievements of the dead person, and associates this with the change from medieval to Renaissance values

Wilson, C., 'The Medieval Monuments', in *A History of Canterbury Cathedral*, ed. P. Collinson, N. Ramsay and M. Sparks, Oxford, 1995, pp.451–510 – a specific study exploring many issues that have implications for tombs and monuments elsewhere in Europe


THE REFORMATION

This is really beyond the scope of this book, but the following titles may be useful to those interested in pursuing the subject further.

Koslofsky, C.M., *The Reformation of the Dead: Death and Ritual in Early Modern Germany 1450–1700*, New York, 1999

Marshall, P., *Beliefs and the Dead in Reformation England*, Oxford, 2002 – two useful chapters, one on pre-Reformation belief and another on the Reformation itself

Reinis, A., *Reforming the Art of Dying: The ars moriendi in the German Reformation*, Ashgate, 2006

# Index

**Acknowledgements**

Production of this short book has depended on a great many people,
many of them colleagues at the V&A. I am particularly grateful to
Norbert Jopek, Liz Miller, Peta Motture, Rowan Watson and Paul
Williamson for reading various versions of the text. Father Rupert
McHardy, at the London Oratory, also read the text and made several
useful suggestions. Lesley Miller and Richard Mortimer helped to
answer specific queries. Of course any errors that remain are solely
the responsibility of the author.

I was lucky enough to enjoy a part-time secondment to the V&A's
Research Department, providing me with valuable time to research
and write the text. Katy Temple, the V&A Photographic Studio and
the V&A Publishing Department have put a great deal of effort into
obtaining the various photographs.

And the greatest thanks go to my family, Richard, Freddie and of
course Arthur, whose arrival during the writing of this book provided
a welcome counterbalance to the subject matter under examination.